M000208268

NURTURING YOUR CHILD'S POTENTIAL

Nurturing Your Child's Potential

How to Make the Most of Your Child's Emotional, Physical, and Intellectual Promise

Dr. Raymond Mitsch

Servant Publications
Ann Arbor, Michigan

© 1994 by Raymond Mitsch
All rights reserved.

Vine Books is an imprint of Servant Publications
especially designed to serve evangelical Christians.

Published by Servant Publications
P.O. Box 8617
Ann Arbor, Michigan 48107

Cover design by Multnomah Graphics/Printing
Cover photograph by Kotoh

94 95 96 97 98 10 9 8 7 6 5 4 3 2 1

Printed in the United States of America
ISBN 0-89283-821-3

Library of Congress Cataloging-in-Publication Data

Mitsch, Raymond.
    Nurturing your child's potential : how to make the most of your
child's emotional, physical, and intellectual promise / Raymond
Mitsch.
      p.   cm.
Includes bibliographical references.
ISBN 0-89283-821-3
    1. Infants. 2. Child development. 3. Child psychology. 4.
Child rearing. I. Title.
    HQ774.M58   1994
    305.23'1–dc20   94-25573
                                                CIP

Dedication

This book is dedicated to my children—Corrie, Anne, Abby, and Elizabeth—who have been given to us for a short while to walk through life with and learn from.

Contents

Acknowledgments

There is no group of people who more deserve credit for an undertaking like this than my family, particularly my wife, Linda. Her patience with my insane schedule of working during the day and writing at night and on weekends was truly of biblical proportions. Her equanimity in the midst of having a baby and encouraging me along this arduous journey made this book possible.

Although my kids didn't know they were contributing to a book like this (all they knew was that Dad wasn't around very much), they have been my inspiration and have taught me about grace, forgiveness, patience, and true character. Thanks, kiddos!

To my supporting cast–Jennifer Nahrstadt, Ed Smyth, Lou Diaz, and Barry Winchell–I really couldn't have done this without you, guys. Thanks for your belief in me and unwavering faith that I was worthy of this task. God used you to encourage me when I needed it and hold my feet to the fire to stay on track.

My grateful thanks also go to Liz Heaney. Her abilities as an editor and encourager were indispensable in making this book readable. Her balance of constructive feedback and "smiley faces" inspired me toward higher levels of quality and clarity in my writing. You have taught me much about communicating with people through my writing.

Finally, my gratitude is extended to you, my readers, for

entrusting me with your time. I pray that my words will be used by God to inspire you to patience with yourselves as parents and may they give you insight into your children as the gifts of God they truly are.

May your deeds be shown to your servants, your splendor to their children. Psalm 90:16

Am I Courageous or Just an Egomaniac?

Potential: "Existing in possibility: capable of becoming actual." In many ways, that *is* the definition of childhood. Children are living and breathing potential. They are capable of becoming almost anything. It is humbling and frightening as a parent to see what power and responsibility we have for our children. When we try to understand their development and budding potential, it's important to realize that nothing about raising them happens in isolation.

From the moment children enter the world, they are surrounded by people who will seek to mold and shape them into an image of themselves or someone they idealize. Unless we have a plan, or at least an idea of what to expect, it will be difficult to control the myriad influences our children will face throughout their short span of years under our wings. The information presented in this book will help to equip you for the tremendous task of facilitating and developing your child's potential.

In the early stages of a child's development there are elements no one can influence or affect. Children have a set eye color, a predetermined hair color, various levels of innate intelligence, body size, and proportions. These cannot be changed unless there is a major trauma to the body system. There is, however, a more flexible and malleable side of the development process that *is* subject to change and variation. This area encompasses emotional, social, motor, language, and spiritual development. We will examine how you can enhance and participate in these exciting areas of your child's life.

No doubt you have read many books about child development and how to encourage your child. This book will bring a breadth of information into one format. You will find out about physical milestones to look for in your child and how to respond to them in positive ways.

Although it's easy to develop expectations about our children and their behavior, if you've never had a child, you may not know what is a reasonable expectation. If you're already a parent, you may have found that your expectations for your children have produced frustration and conflict. I hope that this book will help you develop a more realistic notion of what a child can do. No matter what group you fall into, you will find ideas about how to encourage children and get out of the way of their budding potential.

Many parents, in their effort to be "good" parents, get overly involved in their children's development. Inadvertently, they hinder what they are trying so hard to encourage.

It's important to remember that from the moment of birth, a child embarks on a journey that will ultimately take him or her away from the parent. That may not seem like an especially profound statement. But I have met too many parents who give lip service to raising independent kids, yet seem to do everything in their power to keep them from growing up.

I'll admit, a child's growing independence is a frightening process—one that threatens a parent's self-esteem. We don't want to see our children stumble and fall. Yet it's essential to realize it's our job to help our kids grow up to become well-adjusted individuals who can cope with the stresses of life. Put simply, we have to work ourselves out of a job.

On the other hand, some parents don't get involved enough. In spite of the fact that children will develop with or without their parents' help, children need direction and nurturance. They can't and shouldn't have to do it alone. They need to be guided into healthy lifestyles and relationships.

Parents bent on their children's independence, who always let their children "take their lumps," make as serious a mistake as parents who get overly involved. Developing a child's potential requires patience, balanced involvement, flexibility, and a long-range view of the goal.

You will notice two recurring themes in this book—balance and relationship. Both are vital to ensure that children develop to their greatest potential.

Balance is a difficult concept to express in a few words, especially when it comes to encouraging healthy development. There are many attitudes and actions we must balance in our parenting, including firmness and kindness, encouraging children to try new things without pressuring them to perform, encouraging them to test their newfound abilities, and setting limits on things that are dangerous.

One reason it's so difficult to maintain balance is that it requires making decisions when we'd rather just let things happen. Many parents go to extremes. For example, parents who allow their children to make all their own decisions do so to avoid taking responsibility. If anything goes wrong, they can chalk it up to giving their kids the necessary experience to help them grow. The problem is, these kids suffer from a lack of direction.

On the other hand, parents who make all the decisions and leave none to their children avoid worry by controlling everything. They justify this harmful approach as looking out for their children's best interests. This book strikes a balance between both of these approaches.

The other theme we will discuss is the parent/child relationship. Children develop in a positive way within the confines of a healthy relationship with their parents. Without this relationship, they die both physically and emotionally.

During World War II, many children were left orphaned because of the bombing in London. Although the children had enough to eat and a bed to sleep in, the overextended nursing staff was unable to meet the children's needs for nurture. It was as simple as not having a warm body to touch and hold them. An alarming number of the children died from a lack of emotional bonding.

Time and again, I have been convinced that relationship is necessary for children to grow and learn the essentials of healthy living. A formula I have often used to illustrate this truth to parents goes like this: *Rules + Relationship = Understanding of self, Security with others, and Acceptance of authority.* Our children learn to accept appropriate authority without rebellion in the context of their relationship with us. We help them learn values, learn to think and make decisions, and learn how to handle their emotions. Relationship is the vehicle by which they develop into well-adjusted and principled people. They learn the necessary knowledge and confidence to tap into their potential in proportion to the extent we provide them a safe place to grow.

Our relationship with our children is also the means through which they learn to cope with their own limits. Eventually, we all come to understand the limits of our abilities. We come face to face with the painful realization that there is always someone who is better than we are in almost anything we do. Within the boundaries of a healthy parent/child relationship, children learn to accept themselves—limits and all.

Parenting is a big job, isn't it? Sometimes I wonder if I'm not some kind of egomaniac to think I can actually help someone else become a healthy, adjusted, godly individual. I was reminded of this one day as I sat working on this book. Corrie, my oldest daughter, brought one of her little friends to where I was working. In unison, they walked over to my desk as if they were visiting a display in a museum. They stood quietly and watched as I busily pounded out sentences on my computer keyboard. After an appropriate amount of time, Corrie proudly gestured my way and politely whispered, "Shhhh. My dad is writing a book about kids." The magnitude of such an undertaking was lost on her friend. But I was overwhelmed by the job I had taken on to be her parent.

No doubt about it, we parents are undertaking an ambitious endeavor to help our kids grow up to be capable of adapting to the world without conforming to it. We can have no higher goal as parents than to develop people who can think for themselves and take pride in their value as human beings created in the image of God.

Join me on a journey through childhood. Enter into the wonder, joy, and pain of helping your child grow to live without you. Remember, dear parent, if you do your job well, your child will never be without your legacy and heritage of faith, emotional stability, and personal wholeness.

Chapter One

Following Our Roots

I had just finished my talk about parenting younger children, and the usual number of people came up afterwards to ask questions. One woman in particular caught my attention. She was young and well-dressed; her demeanor betrayed a struggle with anxiety.

"I don't understand it," she said in a shaky voice. "I swore that I would never be like my mother, but one day last week as I was disciplining my boy, I realized that I sounded just like her. My heart sank as I realized what was happening. What you said about our tendency to follow the 'roots' of our own family is true."

"What do you mean?" I asked.

"My parents were always yelling at us. It seemed like we couldn't do anything right. After a while, my brother quit trying. I did just the opposite. I tried harder, hoping that eventually I would get it right. Unfortunately, I'm still trying. My parents' evaluation of me as a parent is a haunting thought every time I try to discipline my son," she said.

I could tell this was going to take longer to explore than we had time for right then. I suggested we get together later to talk about it. When she came to my office, she continued her story.

"My parents were very protective. Both my mom and dad were always keeping track of me, and it seemed like they did everything they could to make sure nothing happened to me. There was little that escaped their attention," she reported.

"Everything I did reflected on them, and they seemed to take everything personally. If I did badly in school, it was as if they had done badly. I felt responsible for their feelings, yet there didn't seem to be anything I could do to make it any better," she said.

"So, how do you see this pattern affecting how you parent your son?" I asked.

"I guess what scared me was that I got frustrated when I didn't get what I wanted from him, and I felt like a total failure. He wouldn't listen to me, and he kept on doing what I told him not to do. I was sure that if I couldn't get him to obey me, I was going to be judged a 'bad' parent. From there, I went into a yelling routine reminiscent of my mom and how she had handled my failures. The problem with my behavior wasn't so much that I had done something wrong. But in her eyes, I was hurting her for having such problems," she said with pain etched all over her face.

"Now I could see those same feelings in me. My child and his behavior were a reflection of my 'grade' as a parent. That was when I started yelling at him. I worried that others would think I was a bad parent. They would think I couldn't handle my child like I should," she concluded.

I now understood her desperation. She had sworn she would never be like her mother, but suddenly she found herself doing the same things to her son that her mother had done to her.

A FORCE TO BE RECKONED WITH

As we begin to explore how to help our children be the best they can be, we need to understand the forces that act upon them. One of the most significant forces is the expectations of the child's parents. Sometimes, these are virtuous and worthy goals that prepare the child to become an independent, well-adjusted individual. Other times, these goals focus on the parents' needs, and the parents "live through" the child, vicariously gaining approval and affirmation through the child's achievements. Ultimately, this results in an entanglement that stunts and hinders the child.

On the other hand, children are not passive victims. They respond just as forcefully to their reality. I'll never forget one of the first nights home with our baby daughter. She had just been fed, yet she was inconsolable. To my adult mind, there was nothing for her to be upset about—her diaper was clean, she had a full tummy, and she had her daddy near, frantic to quiet her. What else could a kid want? She just kept crying.

Ultimately, she and I both survived the ordeal, but I learned an important lesson. I had an eight-pound tyrant running my life and emotions, and I didn't like it. She couldn't tell me what she needed—I had to guess. If her needs weren't met, she would let us know about it. Her insistence would also change me while I attempted to change and train her. I could see it would be push and pull all the way.

The child and the parents make up what I call the "family context." An important part of this context is the parents' relationship with the child. This parental relationship provides the medium in which a child grows. In a sense, it provides the laboratory in which children learn all sorts of things about life that are fundamental to their relationships, values, self-worth, trust, motivation, and understanding of who God is and why he is important to us. Over time, this context fosters certain rules and understandings about how people interact with each other.

Moses understood this context only too well. He knew that God was gracious, but he also knew that we reap what we sow. In Numbers 14:18, Moses reminded God in the face of his wrath over the Hebrews' insolence that "the Lord is slow to anger, abounding in love and forgiving sin and rebellion. Yet he does not leave the guilty unpunished; he punishes the children for the sin of the fathers to the third and fourth generation." In other words, God was totally just and totally merciful and loving. At the same time he loves us, he punishes sin even beyond the limits of the people immediately involved.

While these words may seem harsh and unforgiving, don't lose sight of the fact that they were said in the context of God's forgiveness and mercy. This principle is still true today; we will continue to experience the pain of dysfunctional patterns far beyond the people who instigated them. I don't mean to imply that dysfunctional patterns will be punished, but they are passed on from generation to generation unless we choose to do something about them. When we refuse to confront sin in our homes and families, we feel the consequences.

Parents who want to bring out the best in their children need to be people of transition. This is particularly true if we come from families that struggled in their attempts to rear children effectively. Transitional people are people who mark a change of direction for their family relationships and emotional health. The changes we choose to make will have a lasting effect on our families.

What does it take to be a "transitional person"? It takes an understanding of your roots. You need to understand your history enough to see the kind of changes you need to make. That doesn't mean that you place blame and absolve yourself of responsibility to change. It does mean that you strive to understand the truth about the family in which you have grown up.

You need to take a fearless look into your personal history. If you don't take the time to understand the legacy you bring into your relationship with your children, you are likely to repeat your own parenting history.

Let's begin the process of identifying the legacy of your family relationships.

WHAT KIND OF FAMILY DO YOU COME FROM?

Families come in a variety of shapes and sizes. However, there are certain consistent qualities that set the stage for developing a child's potential. The easiest way to begin to understand family patterns is to answer four questions. Your answers will help you identify how you relate to your children.

How did your parents handle the process of their children growing up and separating from the family? The moment your little one begins to explore his universe, he has embarked on a journey away from you as his parents. This separation is how a child develops his identity. Here are some key questions to help you get a grip on this part of your relationship with your child:

- How do you handle it when your child ventures out on his own—with fear and overprotection, keeping him from doing something he could probably do?

- Do you allow your children to experiment in a safe environment so they can further develop their independence?

- What happens when they express an opinion or thought that isn't necessarily wrong, but is different from yours—do you respond with defensiveness and a cross-examination of the basis for such a thought?

- Do you encourage them to talk about their opinions or thoughts?

If your answers reflect a resistance to your children gaining independence, then you may need to look at this part of your relationship more closely.

How does the family deal with change? I once heard someone say, "The only thing that is constant is change!" Nothing stays the same. We are constantly forced to adapt and develop new rules for relating to each other. For most of us, change is an uncomfortable aspect of our existence. We don't like it, and we often resist it at all costs. This is particularly true when a child enters the family picture.

We like routine in our relationships. Routine makes relationships predictable, and therefore more comfortable. The rub comes when we embark on the process of encouraging our children's potential. Change (or transition) is what helps children realize their potential, and that leaves families in a real quandary. For example, the first child going to school marks a significant shift in family functioning. The family needs to change to adapt to the child's new status. The critical question is: How well does the family adapt to change? Here are a few questions to get you started in identifying how your family of origin dealt with change.

- Did your family meet change with resistance and the denial of a need for change?
- Did change in the family result in disorganization, or did your family maintain stability in the midst of change?
- Did your family insist on keeping things the same because "that's the way we've always done it?"
- Did your family tend to ignore problems until they became crises?

How does the family process information? In other words, how did your family talk to each other? Families have distinctive ways of communicating and understanding each other. This tends to develop over time, and gets more entrenched as time goes on.

Family communication includes how we process information within the family—how we talk to each other, how we listen to what others say before responding, how emotions are handled—and how we process information from the outside—how the family talks about and sees the world.

For example, some families have a distinctly suspicious attitude about the world; they assume that others have malevolent motives and are not trustworthy. Here are some questions to get this aspect of your family relationships into focus:

- Did members of the family neglect to clarify unclear or distorted perceptions of each other?
- Did family members have unrealistic perceptions of each other?
- Did they pigeonhole each other into stereotypical roles and expectations rather than individualized perceptions of each other?
- How did the family handle miscommunication?
- Did they allow each other to "check out" what the other person was saying to clarify the meaning or the speaker's intention?

What roles did each family member assume? Whether we know it or not, we organize the world around us, structuring our relationships in a way that is predictable. The outcome is that we tend to stereotype each other in categorical terms rather than descriptive terms. For example, one person in your family may be characterized as the "emotional" one. Or family members may get upset when someone acts "out of character," assuming another family member's role. Are family members allowed to take on "jobs" that other members do without conflict?

Mary and Don's story illustrates this. Both had grown up in families where the roles of each family member were strictly structured. Although no one talked about it, everyone knew everyone else's role. They knew this by the reaction when someone did another's job!

Mary's father got up early and always prepared breakfast for his family. This was simply his job.

Don, on the other hand, grew up in a family where his mother dutifully and silently got up early and prepared breakfast for the family. He had come to expect this from her. Unlike in Mary's family, this was Mom's job.

You can guess what happened after the honeymoon: both Mary and Don stayed in bed waiting for the other one to get up and make breakfast! Both were surprised to find the other in bed and voiced their discontent that the other didn't know the "job" he or she was supposed to do. Although this is a somewhat comical scenario, it's the hallmark of families that have rigid role expectations for each family member.

Family roles come together to form one of three distinct family patterns. The first pattern is the *enmeshed* family. Enmeshed families do not have clear boundaries between individuals. The members do not have a sense of what each member is responsible for—especially when it comes to emotions.

Boundaries are the invisible lines that mark individual responsibility. For example, members are responsible for the decisions they make, how they express their emotions, how they treat another person, and so on.

It might seem obvious that emotions are an individual's responsibility and no one else's. However, in many families this gets confused and one person's emotions are everyone else's responsibility! When that person gets mad, everyone else gets mad. This occurs in part because the other family members feel it is their responsibility to "fix" what is happening with the upset person. That "fix" may mean cheering him up, telling him to "shape up," listening to his feelings, or just ignoring him.

As parents, we have to be mindful of our children's boundaries and their need for us to stay out and let them be responsible for their own emotions and decisions. To help you figure out whether you came from an enmeshed family, review the checklist below:

1. One or both of your parents were overprotective.

2. Your family couldn't tolerate conflict, and you quickly gave in and apologized in spite of feeling that you had done nothing wrong.

3. One or both of your parents seemed more invested in an extracurricular activity of yours than you were.

4. One or both of your parents seemed to "live through you."

5. One or both of your parents couldn't tolerate your being sad or depressed. Often you may have known this and used it to manipulate them to get what you wanted.

6. You frequently felt that you couldn't discuss anything with your parents without them feeling like failures.

7. Your parents frequently reminded you that your behavior reflected on them.

8. People in your family got offended easily.

9. Your parents often got you to do things by making you feel guilty.

10. You felt you couldn't question your parents' decision without them becoming defensive. (This questioning wasn't to argue with them, but to clarify what went into the decision.) This pattern may still exist in your relationship with them today.

11. You can remember one of your parents searching your room, reading your mail, or listening to your conversations on the phone.

12. Your parents couldn't tolerate your values being different from theirs as you grew older.

(This list is not comprehensive or exhaustive. It is meant to give you an idea of the nature of the family you grew up in.)

The theme of the enmeshed family is: "Be like me; be one with me. You are bad if you disagree with me. Reality and your differentness are unimportant."[1] Although never expressed directly, parents can communicate this philosophy by the way they handle emotions (usually by getting offended or defensive), how they handle conflict (personalizing it as a character assassination), and how they handle thinking that is different from theirs (expressing strongly that this thinking is "wrong"). Enmeshed families can't tolerate individual differences. The progressive growing up of the individual is seen as a threat, and a multitude of obstacles are built to prevent this.

At the opposite end of the spectrum is the *disengaged* family. This family is known by its rigid and separate boundaries between its members. They seem to have little to do with one another.

I counseled such a family while I was in graduate school. The family was composed of an eight-year-old, a mother and father, and three older siblings starting at age eighteen and ranging upward to twenty-five. This poor eight-year-old was outmanned and outgunned by the adults in his family. He had been referred into counseling because of behavior problems at home and at school. At our first meeting, the mother proceeded to tell us how her son's behavior was simply out of control, and that the more adults that were around, the more out of control he became.

Because we were involved in a teaching practicum for family therapy, the student therapists were often called out of the counseling room to be consulted and directed in their strategy in working with the families they counseled. On one occasion with this family, we were called out of the counseling room. While we talked to the teaching team, we watched the family through a one-way glass. As we watched, each family member went to a different area of the room. One adult left to get a drink of water. Another walked to the glass to look out, and another sat and talked with the little boy. It helped us know how to work with this family, because it exemplified their approach with each other. The boundaries between them were so thick and impenetrable that when they had the opportunity to relate, they ran away from each other. They were a perfect example of a disengaged family.

Here is a list of characteristics of a disengaged family:

1. Your family did little together.
2. When you were together, there was an awkward silence.
3. Your parents seemed to have the philosophy that you had to fend for yourself—that was how you would learn to be independent.
4. Your father was absent during your growing up years (emotionally and physically).
5. Your parents seemed more concerned with their fun and good times than with doing family activities together.
6. There was little conflict in your family. There never were enough people around to have conflict!
7. The only thing that brought your family together was a crisis.
8. Your mother or father seemed unaffected by the problems you faced as you were growing up.
9. When your family did get together it seemed like the first chance they got, they would find separate activities (mothers

would talk in the kitchen, fathers watched football, kids went outside to get into mischief).

10. You had little confidence that your parents would really help you in a crisis.
11. You had the overwhelming feeling of loneliness when you were growing up.
12. You seemed to gravitate toward people whom you would or could substitute for your parents.

Remember, disengaged families have boundaries that are too rigid. These walls of steel keep everything and everyone out. These boundaries are so rigid that it takes something major to force family members into each other's arms. By that time, it's too late. By that time, they don't have the skills to relate to each other and the crisis frequently breaks the family apart.

Most families are neither completely disengaged nor completely enmeshed. Families that fit the third pattern often exhibit features of both types. The family that maintains a balance between these features is truly healthy. This family manages the growing up process well and commits itself to the healthy adjustment of its individual members.

A *healthy* family has a sense of emotional closeness that is only possible between individuals who are separate and have clearly defined boundaries between their own thinking, feeling, attitudes, and behavior. This family also manages change and crisis with flexibility. When they face a crisis, they are close in a way that is secure and consistent. On the other hand, the members in this family can tolerate the separateness necessary to be individuals—thinking separately, feeling differently, and behaving differently. A healthy family can deal with conflict openly and honestly. They can tolerate the tension of conflict well enough to talk about it to a reasonable conclusion, including to agree to disagree.

This is hardly a utopian environment. The most important aspects of the healthy family are a willingness to forgive, to reconcile with each other, and to be open. Healthy families understand that there will be mistakes and problems, but they do not "catastrophize" these problems into thinking that the whole family is going down the tubes.

Some characteristics of a healthy family are:

1. Your family could manage conflict without "character assassinations." Members were willing to talk about their differences and listen to each other.

2. Your parents invested themselves in helping you develop the skills needed to survive independently of them.

3. Your family allowed you to have your own feelings without trying to "rescue" you from them.

4. Your family was willing to "check out" what each member said to avoid misunderstanding.

5. Your family members were willing to pitch in for each other, rather than saying, "That's not my job."

6. Your family members didn't stereotype each other, but could see each other realistically with both strengths and weaknesses.

7. Your family members were willing to forgive each other for mistakes and work at reconciling conflicts.

YOUR FAMILY AND YOU

What do these three family models have to do with the way you encourage your children? As I suggested at the beginning of this chapter, we all have the tendency to follow our roots. That is, when confronted with our children and their development, we tend toward that which we know—how we were parented. Without understanding the kind of parenting we received (and its resulting problems), we will be hard-pressed to know how to change our own parenting behavior.

We must approach our attempts at changing these patterns with balance or we will be in danger of committing an opposite error of the pattern we are trying to change. Going in the opposite direction is not the solution. The solution lies in charting a course toward a balanced approach in encouraging our children. The best for our children and the development of their potential starts with us and our relationship with them. It will provide the context they will need to be all that they can be.

If you came from an enmeshed family, you will always need to be on guard for your tendency to confuse the boundaries between you and your child. For example, you may personalize your child's misbehavior into a reflection of your parenting abilities. When this happens, boundaries between you and your child may become a problem.

You will have to learn the hard lessons of allowing your child to choose for himself, even if it means he will choose a way you don't like. You may feel as if you're constantly holding yourself back from helping him to learn the obvious lessons of life. Think back to the effect on you when your parents "saved" you from making mistakes. Did it really help? Didn't you make the same mistakes at some later point?

"But," you might ask, "isn't it showing our children that we love them to spare them from such pain?" At times that may be so, particularly when your toddler is heading for the street at breakneck speed! But when life or limb is not at stake, then you must ask yourself: *Whose pain am I really protecting? Mine or my child's?* All too often, parents interfere in their child's decision-making because they are afraid of the consequences. If the truth be known, we may fear the helplessness we feel when we see our children suffer the consequences of their own actions.

Parents who have grown up in an enmeshed family need to study God's parenting style. Time and again, he showed that he was willing to allow his children to learn from the consequences of their mistakes. If we look at our own lives, we can concur with the observation that God is willing to allow us to make mistakes to teach us the more enduring lessons we need to learn.

When the Israelites complained about having to eat only manna, God's response was: "OK, you want meat, you will have it." God, as the parent, knew they would suffer because of their choice, but he wanted them to learn the hard lesson about complaining and ingratitude. Look at Numbers 11:18-20:

> Tell the people: "Consecrate yourselves in preparation for tomorrow, when you will eat meat. The Lord heard you when you wailed, 'If only we had meat to eat! We were better off in Egypt!' Now the Lord will give you meat, and you will eat it. You will not eat it for just one day, or two days, or five, ten or twenty days, but for a whole month—until it comes out of your nostrils and you loathe it—because you have rejected the Lord, who is among you, and have wailed before him, saying, 'Why did we ever leave Egypt?'"

Let's bring this down to a human parenting level. There are two important issues in this incident. The first was an internal boundary issue—the "right" of the children of Israel to choose. The second was an external boundary issue—the relationship between God and his children. This external issue relates to God's reputation among the nations. God had a reputation to uphold. He knew that other nations were watching, and these nations were afraid of Israel because of his presence and blessing of them.

What I want you to notice is that although God was (and is) very jealous of his name and reputation, he always takes the long view of these aspects of himself. He knows that in the end if he produces character and Christlikeness in his children, ultimately he will be glorified. God was (is) willing to accept the appearance of being "cold, aloof, calloused" with the understanding that by allowing them (us) to choose, he will give them (us) the opportunity to learn about his absolute faithfulness and wisdom on their (our) behalf, and their (our) absolute need of him.

That is our job as parents as well—to focus on the need of our children to learn from their mistakes, taking the long view of their development. Often, we are more worried that it may appear we are being cruel in allowing our children to choose wrongly. However, letting them choose doesn't mean we won't teach them appropriate behavior, or that we let them run rampant without limits. It just means that we won't interfere when they have the opportunity to choose, even though we know the choice they make is a poor one. As long as we are consistent with the consequences, they will learn to choose well.

What do you do if you come from a disengaged family where the boundaries are too separate for the parent to respond to the child's needs? If you come from that kind of family, you may falsely think that allowing a child to "take his lumps" is the way to teach responsibility and prepare him for the future. The problem with this approach is that taking lumps means your not intervening when your child needs your help to learn the skills necessary to take on the challenges of life.

If you come from this kind of family, it's important that you become more active with your children. Occasionally take the extra time to rock your children to sleep rather than just putting them to bed. Take some time to sit and watch them sleep; contemplate the magnificent bundle of potential and love God has given you in each one. Take the time to pray for your baby as you rock him, or wear a rut in the living room carpet as you pace to quiet your little one.

As your child grows older, take the time to tell stories from the Bible of children who had encounters with Jesus, or read to him before bedtime. Whatever form the interaction takes, it's important to remain involved with your child, even if it feels unfamiliar. At times, it may feel as if you are interfering. If that's how you feel, it will probably be just the right level of involvement, considering the family environment in which you grew up.

The most important aspect to remember in counteracting our roots is the need for balance and consistency. This aspect can't be overstated. Families need a balance between enmeshment and disengagement. This balance will help our children understand the effects of their behavior on those around them, keep them trying new behavior, and trying to accept more responsibility.

We must try to keep our hands off when our children practice something we've taken the time to teach them. We need to remember that allowing them to face the consequences of their actions is a good teacher as well.

Finally, we must combine firmness with kindness. Through all our efforts to encourage our children and their halting attempts to grow up, they must have a good understanding of how much we love them—from both our words and our actions. This will provide them with the firm base they need to venture away from us in increasing freedom, autonomy, and responsibility.

Our children may fail to listen to us throughout the years to come, but they will never fail to imitate us and our philosophy of life.

Chapter Two

Welcome to the World!

Teach them (God's words) to your children, talking about them when you sit at home and when you walk along the road, when you lie down and when you get up. **Deuteronomy 11:19**

Now that you've examined your own family history, it's time to look at the first days and months of your life with your little one.

First, you have expectations of what it's like to parent a baby. You may also have expectations about how your child will develop ("She will talk early—I just know it!"). Finally, you have plans for how to help your child develop. That is the focus of this chapter—to help you adjust your expectations and begin to focus on what you can do to participate in your child's development during the first twelve months of life. (For a complete listing of developmental milestones during the first year of life, consult Appendix A.)

I'll never forget the impact of Corrie, our first child, on our lives. As we sat at the dining room table, my wife cried over the dramatic change that had taken place in our relationship. It was an unmistakable loss for us. We had always looked forward to the more "romantic" aspects of babyhood. Now, everything we had enjoyed about our relationship as a couple—the spontaneity, the freedom, even the intimacy—felt as if it had been lost the moment our baby was born. She became the instant organizer of both of our daily (and nightly) schedules. We had a one-day-old time manager! One of us *had* to get up in the night if our daughter cried. We had to reorganize our days to adapt to her schedule of feeding, sleeping, and active times.

Probably the most difficult part of adjusting to parenthood was adjusting our expectations of parenthood. In spite of all the stories we'd heard about how rough the first nights with our baby could be, the first night of lost sleep was discouraging. We consoled ourselves with the thought that our baby was no different from those of the rest of the world, but lost sleep is still lost sleep.

I often remember thinking, *How long is this going to last?* The familiar words of my wife still echo in my mind: "Will this kid ever sleep through the night?" or "Will I ever get a full night of sleep?" Our expectations had been blown apart in a few short weeks.

WHAT WERE YOU EXPECTING?

Parents have innumerable expectations for their baby. These expectations can either make or break the first few days and months after the baby is born. They significantly influence how new parents and their baby relate to each other and the feelings they express in the process.

One set of expectations develops even before the baby is born. Many parents enter delivery expecting it to go smoothly and uneventfully. Instead, the labor is long and sometimes complicated. When expectations about the birth aren't met, parents can project these feelings on the baby (as if the baby caused it!), often assuming that the baby doesn't "like" one or both of the parents ("He likes looking at you more").

They could also secretly not "like" their baby because of how poorly things went during the birth. Of course, we would never admit this to anyone for fear of a negative reaction. However, unmet expectations can contribute to difficulty bonding with your baby.

Often parents are shocked that they don't feel immediate, overwhelming love for their baby. Although these feelings are common and normal, they are still disconcerting. Many new parents fear they don't or won't love their baby. An example of just how common these feelings are can be found in one study reported in the

Journal of Pediatrics.[1] This study involved fifty-four mothers and found that only half of them reported positive feelings for their newborns after birth, and only 13 percent identified any positive feelings as "love." The study found that most mothers took about three weeks to love their babies. The strongest attachments weren't fully formed until the babies were two to three months old.

A more common example of expectations and their effect on attachment between parents and their newborn is the baby's gender. With the introduction of ultrasound equipment, the sex of the baby is often known before birth. Equipment, as well as the technicians who operate it, have been known to be wrong. When this happens, there's profound disappointment for those who have banked on one sex or another. These effects are even more pronounced with families who place a higher value on one sex over another.

This was certainly the case for one family. John had always dreamed of having a son. His wife, Lucy, had simply hoped for a healthy baby. The ultrasounds were inconclusive, and the only thing the couple knew was that their baby was growing at a healthy rate. Everything was going according to schedule. In the absence of contradicting information, John continued to hope. In spite of the warnings by his family and wife, John kept talking about all the things he would do with his new son.

When the birth finally produced a healthy baby girl, John was devastated. He wanted to run away from the cold, cruel reality of this tiny form. To him, a girl would face a world where there were men who could rape her; where there was discrimination because of her sex; where nothing in life seemed fair to him. He often thought that a boy would grow up knowing how to protect himself. He could be "strong," and he could care for others. The birth of his daughter confronted his own weakness and fear of being a daddy to one so "weak." John needed to mourn his dream of a son to be ready to love his little girl. It took some time, but he did it. He was willing to talk about the pain of his disappointment. Now, he's the best daddy around for his little girl. She understands that her daddy loves her, and that no matter what, he will try to protect her against any danger.

John's story isn't an unusual one. No matter what the cause, the best thing parents can do for their baby is to talk about how they feel about the infant with someone they trust. They need to allow themselves to feel just about anything.

It's possible a parent will feel a mix of emotions for some time. None of these emotions will decide the parents' future relationship with their baby as long as they talk about it with someone. This someone can be a spouse or a trusted friend who has had kids and can encourage by saying, "It's OK, I've felt that too. It's completely normal. You're on the right track; just keep going!"

John's story underscores the strength of expectations. It's vitally important that we neither attempt to get rid of our expectations (which would be impossible) nor let them run rampant without confronting the truth of them. The key to dealing with expectations is not allowing them to harden into demands. The longer we have expectations and allow them to remain unchecked or unchallenged, the more likely they will become the only thing we will accept. When reality crashes our little fantasy party, we're devastated and angry. Here is a brief list of some expectations new parents often struggle with:

- The baby's sex
- Length and weight
- Maturity of the baby (born "on time" versus prematurely)
- The nature of the birth process (long and complicated versus "short and sweet")
- The baby's appearance
- How the baby "responds" to the parents
- The baby's temperament
- How others respond to the baby

When you sit together and talk about your wishes and dreams for your child, remind each other that if your child doesn't turn out the way you had hoped, it will be OK. Consider Psalm 139:

For you created my inmost being; you knit me together in my mother's womb. I praise you because I am fearfully and wonderfully made; your works are wonderful, I know that full well. My frame was not hidden from you when I was made in the secret place. When I was woven together in the depths of the earth, your eyes saw my unformed body. All the days ordained for me were written in your book before one of them came to be.   **Psalm 139:13-16**

Be assured, dear parent, that part of the writing of your child's days included who his parents would be. There is no accident in a universe in which our Father cares for his children—both those who are grown and those who are newly born!

IT'S HARD TO GROW UP

The first six months of life are an incredibly important time during your child's development. Dr. Theodore Lidz states emphatically, "During no other period of life is the person so transformed both physically and developmentally" as during infancy.[2] He goes on to say, "No part of his experience will be as solidly incorporated in the individual, become so irrevocably a part of him, as his infancy."[3]

It's difficult to enjoy your child's growing up if you don't understand what's going on. That's the purpose of this book—to help you see what is happening to your child and participate in your child's development.

The first six months of life are crucial, and a great deal of change happens in this short span of time. Before I begin to document the change you will witness, let's look at three important principles of growth and development. These principles will form the framework from which you view and understand the development of your little one:

1. *All physical development begins at the head and proceeds downward.* This is the reason children can hold their heads up before they can sit up. Their neck muscles develop before their arm and back muscles. The head of an eight-week-old fetus makes up approximately half of its length. By the time a baby is born, its head is one-quarter of the body's length, compared with less than 20 percent of the length of an adult.

2. *Development takes place from the spinal cord out to the periphery.* That is why infants can flail away at toys before they can grab them and manipulate them in any meaningful way. The larger muscles of the arms develop before the smaller muscles of the

hands and fingers. Infants' muscles in their shoulders also develop before their arms and hands.

3. *All development takes place from the general, unspecific to the controlled, specific.* I will never forget our amusement in watching our next youngest daughter, Abby, react to her favorite toy when she was an infant. When it came into view, her whole body reacted. Her legs would kick, her face would light up, and her arms would start batting at the toy even before it had reached her. Now when she sees the toy she wants, she screeches with delight and walks toward it with her hands outstretched. Her reactions have gotten much more specific and controlled.

Why is this so important for you to know as caregivers? It means that as you see your child develop and grow, you can understand what your child needs for stimulation and fun. Although babies' rates of growth vary considerably, the pattern follows a predictable course. As you keep track of these developmental milestones, you can appreciate the truly wondrous creation with which God has blessed your family and anticipate what needs your baby will have for safety measures, toys, and the interactions with you that are most meaningful.

This is not meant to be a "cookbook" approach to child-rearing. It is meant to give you the framework from which to understand your child's development.

FROM REFLEX TO RESPONSE

The development of your newborn is an amazing thing. It charts a course from a little bundle of reflexes to responses that are under your baby's control. This progression from reflex to response is marked by a virtual explosion in all areas of development.

The principles of growth explained earlier produce a variety of outcomes. Most noticeable is that your newborn's head and trunk are much larger proportionately than those of older children and adults. For example:

- At birth, a newborn's head and trunk make up about 65 percent of its length, compared with 50 percent of the length of an adult.

- A newborn's arms are so short they can't reach above its head (lift your own arms for comparison).
- In the first year of life, an infant's head is bigger around than its chest. At a baby's first birthday, the average size of its head is about 80 percent of its adult circumference, while its chest measures only 50 percent of its adult circumference.

The heads of all infants grow very rapidly, especially in the first six months of life. In the first year, the average baby's head circumference increases 4.5 inches, compared with a growth of just 3.9 inches from age one to adulthood.

The first year of life is an explosive period of growth for your baby's brain as well. Full-term babies are born during the most important period of brain growth. This span of time runs from the start of the last trimester of pregnancy through the first five months of life. The brain of a newborn weighs about 12.25 ounces, one-quarter of its adult size. In the first year of life, it grows to 31 ounces, two-thirds of adult size. By the end of the first year, every brain cell the baby will ever have has been created.

Your newborn's senses and perception are also under intense construction during the first six months of life. For example, a baby's sense of touch develops from being unable to distinguish between a touch and pain to responding to pain by moving the hand to the location where it hurts.

Vision also develops into the acuity of an adult over the first six months. At birth, infants have very poor visual acuity (as bad as 20/290). They struggle to focus on anything that isn't about eight inches from their eyes, and will have difficulty tracking objects moving through their line of vision. By four to six months, infants have nearly the visual acuity of an adult. They can easily focus on objects at different distances, and they learn the connection between two-dimensional pictures in a book and three-dimensional objects in the world around them. For example, if you "read" a book with your infant over the next six months and begin to name animals in an animal sounds book, he or she will begin to associate these sounds with real objects.

One exciting discovery for our children has been to see a dog in their animal book and then see our golden retriever roam through the living room. Eventually, they could associate the two and understand that the same word applied to each object.

Finally, normal newborns can hear quite well at birth. In the first few days they can distinguish the general direction from which sound comes and they can tell the difference between a real baby's cry and a simulated cry.

ON THE MOVE

Motor development is the term used to describe the increasing levels of control babies have over their bodies. Three specific areas are important: gross motor development, fine motor development, and adaptive behavior. Gross motor development describes the gradual control over the large muscles of the body, including the neck, head, trunk, arms, and legs. Fine motor development is the increasing control over the use of their hands, feet, and other small muscle movements. Adaptive behavior refers to the increasingly complex ways in which children make use of their growing muscle skills to act upon their environment. This includes such activities as swiping at a toy to draw it closer, finding their mouths with a rattle, putting Duplos (the connecting blocks that stick to each other) together to build a tower, or crawling off to find a favorite toy.

Remember, development moves from the head downward. Therefore, the first signs of growth will be an infant's control of its head. If you put a newborn on its back and pull him to a sitting position, you will notice that his head lags behind. This is because the neck muscles haven't developed enough strength to hold the head upright. Once head control is achieved, the next step is sitting upright supported. Of course, this is more complex than it seems. Sitting upright requires control of the head with the neck muscles and control of the back muscles. Beyond this there are developing abilities in arm strength, balance, coordination, and lower body strength.

Next, babies learn to roll over and crawl before taking the ultimate step toward freedom: learning to walk. The ability to ambulate about their environment opens up a new world for children (and of course, new headaches for parents!).

I remember one parent telling me of the remarkable discovery her son had made when he rolled all the way under the dining room table. He was so surprised that he startled himself into crying. Once he mastered the momentum of his lower trunk to roll over, he then began to move forward on his stomach. Finally, he moved to creeping (moving along with his body still touching the floor), and then crawling (moving along on hands and knees).

Fine motor and adaptive behavior development go hand in hand as your little one grows. They are complementary in the sense that one grows out of the other. One set of authors captures the interplay of these two areas of development this way: "Adaptive behavior is the practical result of fine motor development, in the same way that going to the supermarket in a car is the practical result of learning to drive."[4]

Although gross motor development is more exciting to watch, fine motor development and adaptive behavior development are by far more functional. Fine motor development and adaptive behavior are crucial to your little ones learning about the world around them. With adaptive behavior they can manipulate and learn more about how the world works and begin to mentally organize the sensory input from the things they interact with.

For example, one fun activity with your little ones as they grow could be playing with blocks. At first, it would appear that the only thing these blocks are good for is sucking on. Remind yourself, though, that as children mouth every living and inanimate object they can get their hands on, they are exploring the nature of hardness, texture, and other aspects of that block. As they grow and begin to manipulate the blocks more meaningfully, they begin to understand how the blocks fit into space. This understanding can then be used to construct objects such as a tower.

Fine motor development starts in the eyes (part of their head) and moves progressively downward to the hands, and eventually to the feet. By about eight weeks, a baby's hands are mostly open, and infants will begin to discover that these amazing things are part of their tiny world. By twelve weeks, they will have begun to discover they can deliberately bring their hands into their field of vision and explore them with their mouths by sucking on them.

As babies begin to understand that their hands are quite interesting, they will also discover they are useful to bring things closer to them. They will begin to take an interest in objects around them and make attempts to sweep the object toward them with their entire arm.

Between two-and-one-half and four-and-one-half months, babies start glancing between their hands and the object they are trying to get to as if they are gauging the distance between the two. As they practice, they begin to correct the movement of the hand as it slowly approaches the object. Before long, they will finally achieve touching the object they are reaching for. This process of reaching for objects is the beginning of hand-eye coordination.

A BUDDING INTELLECT

This time of your infant's life is also vitally important for intellectual development. One pediatrics textbook suggests that "all of the nerve and brain cells a person will ever have are produced by six months of age."[5]

Probably the most influential figure who advanced our understanding of cognitive development of children was Jean Piaget. Piaget believed that children weren't just passive receivers of information; they played an active role in organizing that information. He developed a theory of intellectual development describing four stages of development that included sensorimotor, pre-operational, concrete operations, and formal operation. Throughout this book we will look at two of these stages: sensorimotor and pre-operational.

The stage of intellectual development during infancy is called *sensorimotor*. This stage of cognitive development covers approximately the time from birth to 18 to 24 months of age. During this stage of cognitive development, your baby will exhibit the following characteristics:

- The ability to integrate information from the senses. In other words, the infant can connect various modes of sensing an object. For example, a bell that rings on his busy box can be heard, touched, and seen.
- The capacity to recognize that objects and people exist even when they can't be seen, heard, touched, smelled, or tasted. This ability is called object permanence. In a scene showing this ability, Piaget would hold an interesting doll in front of the infant and he would reach for it. Next, he would hide the doll

behind a cloth, and the infant would give up the search as if the doll never existed. As your child gains the ability to maintain object permanence, you can hide the doll and he will look for it behind the cloth.

- The ability to imitate others, even when they are not in the room.
- A sense of time that includes the understanding of before and after, not just immediate experience.
- The ability to conceive of goals and to plan and carry out behavior to achieve these goals—such as searching for a favorite toy.

It's important to note that these characteristics are seen throughout this period of your child's first two years of life, although some will appear before others. Don't worry if you don't see them right away. Your child's intellectual development cannot be pinpointed according to some developmental chart. It's wise to remember that development follows a predictable pattern but proceeds at unpredictable rates.

EMOTIONS AND YOUR BABY

I have often heard it said that babies have only three states of emotion—getting ready to cry, crying, and getting over crying! Surprisingly enough, the infant has an emotional life that is evolving into a complex and rich blend of emotions: sadness, frustration, anger, happiness, contentedness, and fear. Initially, your little one will seem to exhibit only one emotion—crying. Soon you will find that an infant's cry means different things. Increasingly, you begin to distinguish more and different emotional responses, and you will come to understand when your little one is more fragile and unable to withstand frustration. There will be other times when your little one will be stronger and more able to handle frustration. If you watch and note these aspects (a journal is a handy place to note these things), you will be more astute in encouraging your baby to try new things.

For example, if your baby is in that fragile state, it's not the time to try a new task like hanging on to a rattle and shaking it. On the other hand, if your baby seems more durable emotionally, then it's time to try new things like putting your baby on his back and letting him work at turning over.

Two critical issues are part of the foundation for a healthy and adaptable emotional life. They form the basis upon which your child's emotional well-being will rest. Now, don't get too anxious about them because I've placed such emphasis on their development. I'm not saying that if something interferes with development in these areas (a severe illness or accident), it will spell disaster. I'm trying to underscore their importance and the need to learn about them to give your children the best possible start in these areas. (We will cover these issues in more depth in the chapters devoted to emotional development.)

The first issue relates to what is called attachment or bonding. The second important issue of emotional development is trust. These issues are intertwined and complex.

Attachment is a critical issue in the development of infants. It is so important that without it they would die. An example of this can be found in a research study that examined what happened to infants who were placed in a foundling home. Their mothers were allowed to stay with them during the first three months of their lives. During this time the infants developed quite normally. Then, for a variety of reasons, they were separated from their mothers and cared for by nurses. Unfortunately, each nurse had eight to twelve infants under her care. The kids were well fed and cared for medically, but received little emotional attention. Because of this situation, 30 percent of them died of malnutrition within the first year. Most of the remaining kids either couldn't stand, walk, or talk by the age of four.[6]

In modern parlance, kids such as these are called "failure to thrive" babies. They fail to thrive because of a lack of attachment to another human being. Children grow on love as well as physical nourishment.

Bonding and attachment build on each other. The bonding occurs during the early moments of life, and lays the framework for further attachment between the child and parent.

Widespread concern over bonding began in the early seventies when pediatricians Marshall Klaus, and John Kennell studied twenty-eight women and their infants at Rainbow Babies and Children's Hospital, McDonald Women's Hospital, and University Hospital in Cleveland. Their research suggested that women who had contact with their infants within one hour after birth and extra contact in the first three days were more responsive to and affectionate toward their infants. They followed up these findings by looking at the children when they were two years old. They found that by this time of life, these mothers talked more to their children.[7]

Of course, the question this raises is: What if the mother doesn't have contact with her infant during the first few hours of its life in the outside world? Will her child suffer? Will she be able to bond with her baby? Or, what if the new mom doesn't feel overwhelming feelings of love and attachment upon seeing her baby for the first time? What if she looks at her newborn and is disappointed? Will those feelings last? Will she "reject" her baby and never bond with the little one?

Our first child, Corrie, was a good case in point. My wife had an exhausting thirty-six hours of labor with our oldest daughter and was so worn out after she was born that she didn't have much "love" to muster. Our little one sucked on my index finger for the first hours of life before she had the opportunity to nurse with her mother. My wife admitted that she was having a hard time "warming up" to our daughter. It was only after she had spent time caring for her and nursing her that intense feelings of love and care welled up for our daughter.

This points out what further research has clarified about bonding and its correlation with the future relationship between mother and child. This research concluded that "studies show that early contact between parent and child does not appear to be necessary for the development of a healthy relationship."[8] It appears there are few in the developmental psychology community who support the extreme notion that bonding in the initial hours after birth is crucial. Clearly there are other equally powerful mechanisms operating during the subsequent months, with "mutual attachment being acquired through multiple experiences including breast-feeding, interaction between parent and infant, and caregiving."[9]

One last comment about attachment and bonding. A disconcerting trend in current psychological literature is the focus on the maternal bonding and attachment to the exclusion of fathers. Don't underestimate the need for an infant to attach to or bond with its father. Thousands, even millions, of kids are growing up without a father—in single-parent homes whether by death, divorce, or being born out of wedlock. Research suggests that those children who grow up with a father not only develop more socially and emotionally, but also intellectually.

Dad, you need time to bond with your little one. Your infant needs it as well. Take time to lay your infant down on the couch or floor and look into her eyes; get her to smile at you; find some ridiculous little game ("peek-a-boo," or "where is [your child's name]?" while covering her face with a blanket or cloth); participate in the bedtime routine by rocking your baby. Be sure to rock your baby face up so you can study her face. All these things will further bond you and your child together. Among the moments of my life I will never forget are the ones rocking my kids and gazing into their eyes before they went to sleep.

YOU CAN'T SPOIL A NEWBORN WITH LOVE

Trust in you as a caregiver is critical to your child's development during the first six months of life. Of course, trust continues to be important throughout their lives with us, but the foundation of it begins during the early months of life.

Erik Erikson, a developmental psychologist, formulated a theory of psychosocial development that underscores the importance of trust.[10] His theory describes our emotional growth in terms of the "crises" we face throughout our lifespan. As we struggle with the challenges these crises present, we learn important things about living with people in adaptable ways. Erikson defined the conflict an infant experiences from birth to twelve to eighteen months as "trust versus mistrust." This means that the infant is learning about the reliability and dependability of his caregivers. As he grows and expresses his needs, the infant is learning just how trustworthy people can be. The role of the parents, therefore, is to create for the infant an atmosphere of safety in which he can count on his emotional and physical needs being met.

The application of this concept of trustworthiness can be taken to dangerous extremes. John and Melissa were an educated couple. John was an engineer, and Melissa a teacher. Both knew the importance of giving lots of love and warmth to their newborn.

The problem was that they went overboard.

After an evening speaking engagement, they stopped me to ask what to do about their baby. They were feeling frustrated that they couldn't seem to get him quieted down sometimes. Their little boy was almost seven months old and was getting very demanding. According to these exasperated parents, he just wouldn't play with the toys they gave him. So his mother couldn't do anything else but spend time with him.

I asked them how they handled their baby's fussy times. They said they did all they could to keep their baby happy and warm. When I asked what happy meant, they replied that they did everything they could to reduce the baby's crying times. It appeared that this child couldn't squeak without parental presence and attention. In their rush to meet his "needs," they had inadvertently interfered with his ability to entertain himself.

Don't misunderstand what I'm trying to express here. Your primary task during the first six months of your newborn's life is to give him or her as much love as you possibly can. You can't spoil a newborn with love. It's important, though, to define what spoiling means. Spending time with your children and interacting with them as often as you have opportunity is not spoiling them. On the other hand, as John and Melissa's example shows us, we must keep a counterbalance as we help them grow. We must lavish them with love but remain mindful of their need to eventually learn to comfort and entertain themselves.

Timing is crucial in this process. You can't expect newborns to entertain themselves, and they can't soak up enough warm fuzzies. Because of this, you will need to do that for them. But as they grow, you will need to notice when they can entertain themselves and give them opportunity to do so. Don't forget that even when they can entertain themselves, they will still need periodic, consistent human interaction and direction.

The essence of parenting is balance between meeting the needs of your children and facilitating their learning to do it for themselves. You can't go wrong giving infants as much love and attention as you can show them, but that doesn't mean being constantly present. As they grow, they will need to understand that Mom and Dad aren't their playthings.

HOW CAN I FACILITATE MY BABY'S DEVELOPMENT?

Research makes painfully clear that infants can't get enough love and nurturance from their parents. This helps them to grow almost as much as does the nourishment they receive from food. Be generous and effusive in expressing your love for your child. Enjoy him as he grows and revels in the expanding world of his parents and home.

Also, surround your newborn with toys. Toys are a way to give your baby the idea that the world is a fascinating place to live in and is worth exploring. Remember that toys are the "baby tools" he will use to explore his environment and learn how to interact with it. He has "kid work" to do, and these tools will help him accomplish that work.

The size of your toy budget does not correlate with your child's later IQ. Toys can be something as simple as a wooden spoon or a coffee can with objects in it to shake. Include toys with a variety of textures (soft rubber, hard plastic, or wood), a variety of shapes, and toys that can be chewed. If possible, hang toys from a toy bar.

Here is a sampling of toys most recommended by developmental psychologists:

Mobiles. The characteristics of the best mobiles are:

- A strong contrast of bright colors, and tilted in a way that the baby can see the objects.
- Ability to move so that the infant begins tracking objects with his eyes.
- Adjustable height. A mobile that places the objects beyond the focus length of your baby is useless. The ideal length is 7–8 inches away from your baby's face. As your baby grows you can move the mobile further away so that he can't grab it and pull it down on himself.
- A negotiable characteristic, although it is worth the cost, is a mobile that includes a simple tune. The auditory stimulation begins to open the world even wider for your little one.

Books. This may be a little surprising on a list of toys for newborns, but what better way to provide colorful things to look at than through this format. Board books, which have sturdy pages that can be easily turned by your baby, often portray objects in primary colors. The text is usually simple or nonexistent (wordless). Books allow interaction between baby and parent—not only your presence, but your voice. Some of the latest research into what characteristics separate families with gifted children from other families finds that the parents read to the children right from birth. Look for books that have sturdy pages (heavy cardboard) and can be easily turned by your baby as he grows.

Baby Mirrors. One of the most fascinating things for a baby to look at is the human face. By about four months, your baby will enjoy watching his reflection in a mirror. Our kids carried on in-depth (philosophical, no doubt!) discussions with themselves by looking in their baby mirror.

Toy Bars. A toy bar looks like a miniature swing set with hooks on which to connect loops to attach toys. Toy bars are almost indispensable for keeping a baby stimulated and happy from birth until he can sit up on his own. The toy bar also allows some freedom for the parent to do things independent from the baby. Toy bars allow your child to experiment with eye-hand coordination.

Rattles, clutch toys, squeeze toys. The old standbys are as important as ever. Your baby is born with a grasp reflex that makes him clench his fist when his palm touches an object. This reflex will fade in the first few weeks of life and he will keep his hands open more of the time when he's awake.

Over time, your baby will begin to move into the next stage of motor development which includes grasping an object and reaching for it. You can help in this development by having toys available for your baby to grab. He won't have any idea he is hanging on to something until he accidentally shakes it. That's how he learns a little more about his expanding world.

Cognitive development and social and emotional development depend on interaction between parent and child. Research shows that children who are played with and who engage in other activities with their parents develop these skills more quickly. Although children are not passive recipients of culture and wisdom, it's important to remember that as you interact with your child, he is learning a little bit more about the world. Your home is his laboratory to experiment and learn.

Another thing you can do to help your child's development is watch your boundaries with him. I have seen too many parents attribute adult motives to infants—"He's just being stubborn!" or "He's just trying to be defiant," or "He's trying to make me mad!" This is a dangerous tendency. In fact, studies of child abuse suggest that some people end up abusing their children because they attribute adult motives to child behavior. Don't get me wrong; I am not saying that if you do this you are on your way to becoming a child abuser! What I am saying is that the crux of the problem with an infant's behavior is with the parents. We might believe that our children's behavior reflects on our parenting skills. For example, you may feel that your child is not eating well because you are not a good parent. You may reason: "If I were a good parent, my child would eat well, be happy, and rarely cry."

We must be careful to be accurate in our assessment of infant behavior. Remember that infants don't have the cognitive abilities to be vindictive or even demanding (although it may look that way). Most of what they do is motivated out of a desire to express that something is wrong in their little world. If you have done all you can to comfort them—changed their diaper, made sure their tummies are full, made sure they are warm, given them a nap— then relax and don't leap to a conclusion about the whys of their behavior. Of course, relaxing is tough when you have a screaming baby in your ear. Work to remind yourself that "this, too, shall pass," and that as you work to meet their needs, they will quiet down.

Finally, pray for your child as you put him to sleep at night. It's easy to be put out by the interruptions and "demanding" nature of your infant. One thing that will refocus those thoughts is prayer. It is my contention that the beginning of spiritual development of your child begins with your prayer life for him.

We have done that with our girls. As a matter of fact, one of the first words our oldest daughter learned to say is *amen*. She learned it from hearing her mom and dad pray for her as they put her to sleep. It had become as much a part of her bedtime routine as rocking.

We all enter parenthood with high hopes for a bright future for our children. As we grow together, there will be a lot of things to temper our expectations. This can either produce disappointment or help us to become more realistic. *Adjust* and *adapt* are the key words for this period of your child's life. That doesn't mean you are settling for mediocrity. It means that you are learning and so is your child.

Your Child from Six Months to Two Years

Chapter Three

Did You Hear That?

Imagine a scene with me. We're standing in a labor and delivery room witnessing the most dramatic moment in all of life—the birth of a child.

"Hang in there, honey, you're doing fine!" the husband encourages.

"Here comes another one," the woman warns the participants.

"OK, get ready to push," the doctor instructs, sitting in front of the woman in a catcher-like pose.

"DEEP BREATH. NOW PUSH!" the doctor continues.

The husband leaps into action, "1... 2... 3... 4... 5... 6... 7... 8... 9... 10. OK, honey, breathe. One more time! 1... 2... 3... 4... 5... 6... 7... 8... 9... 10. Good... good, here comes the baby!"

His counting is punctuated by the cries and groans of his wife as she pushes the baby down the last short distance to its new life with them.

"OK, deep breath." The doctor senses the imminent contraction. "Now... P U S H!"

The husband counts as his wife screams in pain and anticipated joy.

"You have a boy!" the doctor proclaims, holding the little one high enough for the proud parents to see their progeny. He promptly cuts the umbilical cord and places the little one on his mother's tummy. The baby cries in an unknown environment he never knew existed.

"Hello, my little one! We have waited so long for you. Welcome to our family. You have some very excited brothers and sisters waiting for you!" The mother coos in a hushed voice, understanding only too well the miracle of life and relationship.

It is a cataclysmic moment few ever forget. Recently we welcomed our fourth daughter, Elizabeth, into the world. We welcomed her with words of love and warmth. We didn't "know" this new member of our family, but we didn't need to. She was part of our family even before we knew her personally. Yet we talked to her—even though she didn't have a clue what we were saying. It happened spontaneously, naturally. Our voices were comforting to her as she quieted to listen to this new and strange sound she had heard only in muffled tones in utero.

This natural inclination to speak to our baby is what we build upon in helping our children grow in the use of their language and communication. To newborns, the voices of their mother and father are the most attractive sounds they can hear.[1] Our voices calm our babies' cries and produce the most interest in them as they turn their heads toward it. Our voices speak comfort and peace to them in the days ahead as they struggle with their new world.

HOW DOES LANGUAGE DEVELOP?

Children develop gradually in their capacity to understand and use language. Essential to the development of language is the ability to hear yourself and those around you. We've been designed so that we need feedback from our environment to survive. This is particularly true in the production of speech. Researchers have found that by three months, deaf babies begin to stop making noises and other vocalizations because they can't hear themselves.

Approximately 50 percent of children identified with hearing loss give no clues other than behavioral ones that lead to a suspicion of hearing loss. The other 50 percent give clues that should alert parents and professionals to the potential development of hearing loss.[2] The following chart lists hearing milestones you can expect of your child, and some age-specific suggestions you can try to encourage communication at these ages.

Birth to three months:
- Startles to sharp clap within three to six feet
- Can be aroused from sleep with sounds only
- Cries at sudden, loud noises (door slamming, dog barking)
- Ceases crying to a loud sound
- Reassured by laughter and sounds of pleasure
- Calms to voice, appears to listen
- May coo when being talked to
- Displays taking-turn skills vocally
- Contrasting sound attracts attention

At this age you can talk to your baby, and notice the "taking turns" aspects of his auditory development. It may sound ridiculous, but carry on a conversation with him. Tell him all about what you are doing (changing his diaper or what he is seeing). His only response may be a coo or some other vocalization, but that's OK.

Another characteristic is contrasting sounds. Your baby will notice changes in starting consonants, such as "ba-ba-ba-ba" changing to "pa-pa-pa-pa." Not only is this entertaining, it will give you a clue to the sensitivity of your baby's hearing.

Three to six months:
- Recognizes mother's voice
- Enjoys own body noises (crying, lip buzzing, tongue clacking)
- Laughs, coos, and babbles for pleasure
- Begins to turn head toward sounds
- Perceives rhythm, intonation, duration, and frequency of sounds
- Responds to loving or angry tones of voice
- Localizes to soft speech sounds
- May not startle as in the earlier period

Make a habit of talking your way through your day with your little one. Talk to him about everything you do for him. At this age, he is beginning to appreciate your voice and the subtleties in it (intonation, rhythm, and so on). Call him by name and watch him turn to your voice (not to his name just yet).

Six to nine months:

- Localizes on the horizontal plane (In other words, he can figure out where things are in space depending on their sound as long as they are in front or behind him, not above. This is dependent on hearing in both ears.)
- Responds to own name
- Turns to sounds that are at eye level and downward
- Plays pat-a-cake and peek-a-boo
- Imitates sounds and intonations
- Understands meaning of simple words (no-no, oh-oh)
- Gives attention to singing or music
- Recognizes names of a family member even when that person is not in sight

Be sure to play "Where is?" games with various members of the family, including family pets. It will give you a sense of what your little one is beginning to understand. The people can be in or out of the room. Your little one is likely to react either way.

Also, encourage him to imitate the sounds you make—these can include words, which may sound like "sounds" to him.

Connect various actions with words. For example, when he drops something say "Oh-oh." Before long you will notice that he will begin to say it spontaneously when he drops an object.

Nine to twelve months:

- Searches for auditory stimuli (bell or squeak toy)
- Can find a sound behind himself
- Enjoys listening to new words
- Uses first meaningful word
- Begins using conversational-sounding babble with some recognizable words in place
- Points to or looks at a familiar object when asked
- Can wave "bye-bye" to verbal command

Just for fun, hide a squeak toy behind your back and see if your little one tries to find it. Next, put it behind him and watch him wiggle and squirm to see it. It's a fun game, and one that will tell you a lot about his hearing. Continue the "Where is?" games to build his familiarity with words and their objects. Whenever people arrive, practice saying "hello" or waving "hi!" When they leave, wave "bye-bye."

As parents, we are the most attuned to our children's abilities. Many studies have found that parents suspect a hearing loss as much as 12 to 14 months before any formal testing is done.[3] Therefore, it's important to take such a list and notice how your child hears you and the sounds in your home. As with any list of characteristics, there is a wide variability in children's ability and sensitivity. If your child's behavior doesn't match one or two things on the list, don't worry. Only a general pattern of absence of these behaviors is important and should arouse concern and a consultation with your pediatrician.

Assuming your child can hear adequately, and has passed through the expected milestones of auditory development, the first aspect of language development you will notice is called *receptive language.* You can see this developing ability when you give instructions to your child to get something for you. We noticed it most when we asked our youngest daughter, Abby (before our most recent birth), to go and get a favorite book of hers, and she understood! It was surprising to see that she understood a simple two-step instruction—get a book and bring it to her parent. You can test children's ability by asking them to get some item for you. You may be surprised at what they understand.

In a more humorous vein, you can always tell the level of receptive language a child has by how his parents talk to each other in front of him. For a long time, we know that what we say is "safe" from listening ears. It has little or no meaning to the child, so we don't have to worry about editing or concealing what we are talking about. But when we detect that we are being understood, we will resort to spelling the words out! It is our way to stay ahead of our children as their increasing levels of understanding move them further and further into our world of communication.

Along with understanding what is said, there is also the understanding of how conversation proceeds. As they grow, children begin to understand the reciprocal nature of conversation even before they can understand the words being spoken around them. For example, at approximately eight months old, babies may begin to take an interest in conversation even though it is not directed toward them. If they are sitting between their parents, they may look as if they're watching a tennis match as they watch the interchange.

As children grow in their understanding of words, they will be able to follow adult conversation. Our youngest daughter often detected when we were talking about the birds at our bird feeder outside our dining room window. Her eyes would light up and she would point out the window. Frequently, whenever she heard someone mention "birds," she would look out the window or go toward it demanding to be lifted to look out the window at the birds.

Productive language develops much later and is marked by your child's first attempts to talk. It requires a vocabulary and an understanding of the rules for speaking. In the beginning stages of this learning process, adults are fairly forgiving with children and their language. The longer children attempt to talk with us, though, the more they find they need to be more precise. This precision is necessary for us to understand them and respond appropriately. Therefore, to be understood, children learn the basic rules of expressing their needs, thoughts, and emotions. This is the basic course that productive language follows as it develops. But why is it so slow to develop?

One reason why productive language develops slowly is that children learn how to communicate their needs without language. Unless encouraged to do otherwise, they continue this form of communication and put off learning to speak. One little boy found he was able to get his parents to meet his needs with a series of grunts and gestures. His parents, in their rush to be "good parents," would get what he wanted. If this didn't work, the one word he did know and use was "NO!" Note that he used a word but only when he needed to. Need is a great motivator!

Also, if children are growing up among older siblings, this ability will be slower to develop because they have to compete for "airtime." Not only that, their older siblings are not likely to make them talk to get something. Older brothers and sisters, like their parents, have learned to interpret their gestures rather than making them talk to get what they want.

Until children reach the age of two, their receptive language is a better measure of their language ability than their productive language. While my eighteen-month-old may have a vocabulary of thirty to seventy spoken words, her understanding of the words I use with her may very well be twice or three times that number.

FROM "GOO" TO "BLUE!"

Many parents believe their child's first words mark the beginning of his language development. As a matter of fact, your child's speech has begun much earlier than that. The foundation for it has been laid before the first distinguishable words are ever spoken. Early speech is just one step in the complex process of communication that begins when a child is born.

The first step in this journey is your baby's first sound. Your baby's cry is the most welcomed sound at birth. We all look forward to that sound as an indication of health. Somewhere along the way, though, this same crying behavior becomes unnerving to parents. Yet, an infant's cry is his first rudimentary form of communication and a clue to what is going on internally.

During the sixties, researchers found auditory differences among the first birth cries and subsequent cries of hunger, pain, and pleasure, and between the cries of sick and healthy infants.[4] Since then, further research has found distinct differences to be related to an assortment of physical problems including Sudden Infant Death Syndrome, premature birth, brain damage, and birth complications.[5]

Crying also serves another purpose. Crying helps children to become aware of their jaws, palate, lips, tongue, and most important, their voice. It provides them with auditory feedback vital to adjusting their vocalizing behavior to be heard and understood.

Somewhere between six and eight weeks your infant will begin to make noises that resemble vowel sounds such as oohs and aahs. These cooing sounds are the basic building blocks for what will come later.

As our family begins another journey through life with our fourth daughter, one distinctive thing about her is the "humming" she did even at a week old. She is already beginning to make noises that clearly seem to show her pleasure, although we know there is no such meaning attached to it by her. She hums when she is nursing. Her sense of rhythm is most exquisite (spoken like a true father!) and keeps pace with her nursing and swallowing. These sounds and the many others she will begin to make are the first attempts at interacting with the world around her.

Around six months of age or later, your baby will begin to babble. Babbling consists of repeated consonant-vowel combinations such as "ba-ba-ba." Initially, they are not produced with any meaningful intent. It's almost as if infants are playing and experimenting with sound. They are interacting with themselves as much as they are with the world around them. These sounds are common among babies all over the world, but within another month or two, they will begin to babble in their native language. They will drop the sounds that aren't used in their language, and their intonation and rhythm will begin to resemble that of their native language.

Babbling progresses to *jargoning,* which sounds like sentences made up of nonsense syllables. It is at this point that languages begin to diverge—jargoning is different in every language but sounds like the native language. It is during this stage of children's language development that they will begin to show more interest in adult conversation.

The ninth month marks the beginning of an exciting spurt of your little one's attention to sound and language around him. Your baby's form of speech becomes more elaborate, with a drawn out series of syllables being produced such as "loo-loo-loo-loo." Also children begin to inflect and change the emphasis of their sounds. Often, their listening parents will hear a variety of sounds that suggest questions, exclamations, and commands. This development of more elaborate forms of jargoning begins to sound so realistic that you swear your children are speaking in another language. During these times, you may think that if you knew their language you would understand exactly what they were saying!

The culmination of this long, arduous process of producing speech is found in your child's first word(s). Most babies produce their first "real" word between the tenth and twelfth months. This is sometimes difficult to pin down since the distortion of these words is immense.

One of our daughter's first words was our dog's name. As I was looking for an example of the kind of distortion you can expect, I listened in one day to our next youngest daughter as she tried to get our dog's attention. She had decided to get Sunny to obey her. As she looked at our dog with intense concentration she began her command with "Shi-sha!" and then some garbled string of words. She was obviously mimicking Mom and Dad as they got Sunny to obey (we initiate a command to the dog by her name). Surprisingly, Sunny "knew" what to do, because Abby had come close enough!

As your children's increasing knowledge of their world develops, their attempts to express their thoughts and feelings about it will increase as well. Between twelve and eighteen months of age, your little one begins to put words together in simple two-word sentences. These sentences are shortened versions of what they are obviously trying to say. For example, your child may have put together the words "Mama bye-bye?" This question can mean "Mama is going bye-bye," or "Bye, Mom," or even "Is Mama gone?" These are called *telegraphed* sentences. They are condensed versions of what is really meant. It is an economical way to speak when your vocabulary isn't broad enough to express your thoughts.

By age two, children will begin to expand their sentences to be more specific. Their sentences will move from two-word to three-word sentences. These rudimentary sentences are still telegraphed but are closer to expressing the exact meaning the child has in mind. The above question of "Mama bye-bye?" will be turned into "Mama go bye-bye?" This question is specific enough to express the child's question about Mom's presence or absence.

From eighteen months and beyond, your child's vocabulary will explode, and you will find yourself hard-pressed to keep up with your list (if you are keeping one). It has been estimated that "the average child learns at a rate of five thousand words per year, or about thirteen per day."[6] Probably the greatest increase comes from eighteen months to three years.

TALK TO YOUR NEWBORN

What can you do to encourage your child's language development during the first two years of life? Do what comes naturally to you—talk! Lots of loving talk about anything is the best help you can give to your baby's language development. Here are a few specific things you can do:

Talk directly to your baby. If this is your first baby, this suggestion won't be a problem. You will probably be talking to your baby all the time. As more children are added to the family, it's easy (take my word for it!) to lapse into talking from afar in the hope that your baby will be consoled that you are at least in the room. Practically speaking, this will often affect the timing of later children's language development. Many third and fourth children are often delayed in their speech development because they get so little one-to-one, face-to-face interaction with an adult.

A baby cannot pay attention and listen carefully to general conversation. You must find a way to secure his attention and hang on to it. Our youngest is pretty challenging in terms of getting her attention because her little neck muscles haven't developed enough to keep her head still. Therefore, her head wags from one side to another as she tries to focus on whomever is talking to her. At times I have had to put her down in her infant seat so that her head rests on the back of the seat. Then, as she scans for me, I can catch her eye and do something silly to keep her attention (smiling really big and exaggeratedly, or making some noise with my mouth).

Other opportunities to talk to your baby include the daily routine (taking a bath, changing a diaper, feeding times). Babies may be the most alert when they first wake up. Catch their eye and engage them in making noises and other cooing sounds. Increasingly, their ability to imitate you will improve and become a fun game between the two of you. As you catch their attention, you can talk more to them as their interest increases. As babies listen to us they become accustomed to the intonations and rhythm of language.

Read to your child. Reading books is an effective means to enlarge your child's world of language. One researcher remarked that reading was so critical to language development that she recommended children hear "at least a book a day from the age of six months on."[7] This practice also helps your child understand that the written word stands for a spoken word. Although they don't understand what is being said to them, they will grow accustomed to language and its symbolic nature. Before long, they will understand that something on a page can symbolize something that is being said.

Let your child talk while you're reading. It has long been established that reading and language development are connected, but researchers have found another important element in the equation of language development—allowing your little one to interact with you over the pictures you are looking at in a book. Initially, this means that you will name and talk about the pictures in the book you are looking at together ("This is a cow, and here's a house, and look, here is a pig!"). Remember, any time spent looking at pictures and naming what you see is adding to your child's comfort with language and exposure to the use of words.

As they grow in their use of sounds and words, they will begin to make sounds in anticipation of the pictures in your book. Our next youngest daughter still does this even though she knows the words to describe certain animals. I think she likes to make the animal sounds more than using the words. You can further engage children in this process by asking, "What is this?" and see if they will make the sounds for the animals pictured.

Finally, as their ability to express their thoughts improves, you can begin to ask them questions about what is pictured in the book you are reading. You can do this while you read the book to them. Then, as they answer, you can expand what they are saying. As you do this you will be expanding their language use, making book reading an interactive, participatory activity rather than a passive exercise in listening.

As your child's speech increases from ten months and into his second year of life, encourage him to use his newfound language skills to ask for things rather than gesturing. Your little one has no doubt learned how to grunt, whine, or otherwise gesture either by hands or body. This has been acceptable, since he hasn't had the knowledge to express his thoughts through words. The next time he gestures for something you know he knows how to name, ask, "What do you want?" If he names the object, it will tell you he can express his thoughts to get this object. It will also mark (for you and your child) the beginning of your efforts to help him use words for what he wants.

This is also a time to teach the use of words for manners. Often among the first words our children learn are "please" and "thank you." As frequently as you think of it, ask for a "please" before giving an object to your little one. One of our daughter's best approximations of thank you was "Ank ou, Mama!"

Increase feedback. Respond to recognizable consonant-vowel sounds such as "mama" with "Mama is here." Remember the importance of feedback? We can't adjust our vocalizations without feedback (or without hearing what we are saying). As our children develop their language skills, we have to be the ones to give them the feedback they need. Eventually, as they begin to make sense of their own sounds and vocalizations, they will use their sounds as the basis to create more language. Until that happens, we are their means of understanding what they are trying to say (sometimes they may know, and other times you can further develop words for them by giving them words to express an idea).

Another error parents make in providing feedback to their kids is talking to them in "baby talk." Be sure to talk in your normal language. Don't lapse into baby talk. Baby talk is not mimicking an infant's consonant-vowel sounds. Baby talk is the adult caricature of baby sounds and vocalizations. If you are in the mood for fun, it's OK, but if you are trying to develop a pattern of encouraging your children's language, don't change your language pattern for them. Let them get used to yours and be the ones to mimic it.

Finally, engage in the exercise of expanding their shortened phrases and two-word sentences. For example, if your little one asks for a cookie by saying "gookie?" you might respond with the question, "You want a cookie?" Be profuse in your expansion of their words and phrases. This teaches them more in each situation even if they don't completely understand.

AVOIDING THE COMPARISON GAME

In the face of pressure to keep up, we need to maintain the middle ground between pushing our children to say their first words and engaging in "benign neglect" by allowing them to say their first words whenever they are ready to do so. Language is both caught as well as taught. Yet the rate of development varies widely among "normal" children. One author related this humorous but revealing anecdote about an unfortunate parent who tried too hard to develop her child's language.

I once observed a young mother diligently attempting to induce her one-year-old to say his first words. Over the course of the previous few months, she and her husband had been urging the child to say "Mama" or "Dada" on a regular basis. On this particular day, she was kicking the effort into high gear.

As this woman moved about the kitchen preparing the evening meal, she repeatedly passed in front of the infant who was propped in a seat nearby. Each time she captured his attention, she would lean forward and cajole, "Say Mama... say Mama." However, despite her perseverance, her overtures continued to be met by a cheerful but silent smile.

Then all of a sudden, while transferring a dish from the stove to the table, she accidentally spilled some hot gravy that splattered across the floor below; and without thinking she let out a loud "Shoot!" To her surprise and chagrin, the infant looked up, smiled again, and repeated "Shoot!"[8]

Unfortunately, this parent interfered with her child's first words because she was so intent on getting him to talk.

Another principle to keep in mind: Don't get caught up in the comparison game. It will lead to disaster as you are trying to help your child expand his world of language. One mom came to me extremely upset. She was sure that her Tommy was "developmentally delayed." After talking with her for a time, I realized she was comparing Tommy with someone. I asked, "So tell me, who are you using as a comparison for your son?"

She looked at me as if I were asking something that was entirely irrelevant. "My sister's boy is only a few months older than my boy, and he is doing so well with language."

"Tell me about him," I requested.

"Well, he is an only child and my sister's first. It doesn't look like she is doing all that much with him, but he is talking so much more than Tom," she said.

"Comparisons are funny things," I said. "When we make comparisons we sometimes have a hard time finding a suitable comparison. Therefore, we look for a person who is the way we want to be—like you have done with Tom. You would really like him to be as verbal as your nephew. What's unfair is that your nephew is older than Tom and an only child. Tom is your second child, and your older child is a real talker. It is quite natural that Tom is going to be a little slower in developing his language. Because of whom you are comparing him with, it is a comparison he will inevitably lose at this age."

When we compare our children with other children, the only one who loses is our own children. Their uniqueness is lost in the sea of developmental conformity to which their understandably anxious parents are trying to adhere. The key to making the process of learning to talk as enjoyable as possible is not to push the process. It is essential to remember that for any educational experience to be effective, it must be done in an environment of acceptance (allowing for mistakes), and you must be tuned in to your child's interests and abilities. Pushing the process of learning language too hard or too soon may initially produce spectacular results, but in the end it will be counterproductive.

Chapter Four

Look Ma!
No Hands!

A parent I talked with related a humorous story of her child's first steps. Her young son, John, had mastered the necessary skills to stand and cruise around the living room by holding on to furniture. When he stood unsupported for the first time, he surprised his parents and himself. He looked at them as if to say, "Wow! How did I do that?" He promptly dropped to his rear to try it again.

John showed a great deal of ingenuity moving through the house without losing steam so that he never had to leave the safety of his handholds. No matter how hard his mom tried to coax him away from his safety zone, he would simply smile slyly and dive into the nearest furniture cushion.

One day, she had been standing in the kitchen talking to her sister on the phone when at the doorjamb she noticed four small fingers grasping the molding. Slowly, around the corner little Johnny appeared, searching for his mom. To her amazement, he let go of the molding and began to toddle toward her. Smiling as if he were in total control, he continued to string together one impossible step after another. With each step and increasing momentum, his face changed from smug contentment to sheer panic and terror. He was picking up speed almost as if he were being propelled by a force he couldn't control. At any moment, he seemed poised to lurch forward into a full-face belly flop on the floor.

"He's walking!" she screamed into the phone, nearly rupturing her sister's eardrum. In that moment, he lunged forward to cling to the safety net of his mother's knees.

"It's a moment I will never forget in all my days," she remarked. "He was so proud of himself, and I was crying with excitement. I guess I was a little surprised by my excitement, but I remember seeing him work so hard to stand up, then finally cruise down the sofa. It was like seeing your favorite person in the whole world get a well-deserved honor."

There are few moments in a child's life that parents remember more vividly than when their children take their first steps. It is a monumental event in a family. Of course, motor development doesn't end with your little one's first steps. This event simply exemplifies what has been happening and will continue to happen for some time.

WHAT CAN I EXPECT TO SEE?

By the time your little one can walk, he has developed a number of skills that ultimately result in walking. In Appendix B you will find a chart that breaks down these skills and stages you can look for as your little one develops this most exciting skill.[1]

As your little one begins to move and explore his world, keep in mind that his motor skills will develop in a stair-step fashion. Development rarely progresses upward in an ever-increasing slope. It comes in starts and stops along the way. As your toddler tries new things, he may regress somewhat. For example, as your child concentrates on walking, he may become more dependent and fragile emotionally. This is to be expected, since he is taxing his immature emotional system in his determined attempt to master a new skill. Fortunately for them, children don't have an understanding of time like we do, or they would choose to crawl the rest of their lives!

As you pour over the developmental milestone charts, be careful that you don't become too rigid about when certain skills are developed. If you do, you will set yourself up for needless worry. This overconcern with norms will also hinder your ability to respond with compassion as your little one struggles for independence.

We must always watch our expectations to make sure they don't dictate to our children how they "should" develop. Their own bodies will dictate the pace. We need to encourage, comfort, and get excited at their determination to move.

When children get frustrated with their inability to walk or move the way they want to, we need to be ready to reassure them they are still OK. If it seems that children are getting so frustrated that their frustration gets in the way of their efforts, they may need a break. Distract them so they can recover before they try again. Of course, the moment I say this I realize there will always be those kids who won't be distracted from the "project" they are working on. In that case, let them work at it until it looks like they are ready for some rescuing. At that point, distract them with a book or some other activity. Remember, motor development is predictable and orderly, but that doesn't mean it is even and proceeds at a smooth rate.

Where does this odyssey toward mobility begin? Babies will begin to look around and realize the world is a really interesting place. Their first movements will include lifting their head and turning the head from side to side in response to an interesting sound. This movement of the head precedes the ability to move the rest of the body in response to something interesting.

As they gain further control over their bodies, their shoulders will rotate with their heads, and before long the rest of the body will follow. Once they can get to their tummies, the next step will be creeping. Creeping is scooting along on the tummy. As they do this, they are using their arms and legs to propel themselves in some direction—sometimes the direction is backwards.

Our daughter Abby had this happen to her, much to her consternation. She had delightedly learned to move her body. Unfortunately, when she was sure she was going to get a toy, she would instead move further away from it rather than closer. It frustrated her and usually resulted in many tears, although to the onlookers (her sisters included) it seemed quite comical. Naturally, it was a joyful day in our household when Abby finally learned to move forward.

The next set of movements occurs around the seventh month and comes in a rapid procession. First, babies creep, then crawl, and then stand. These aspects of motor development clearly show the maturation that takes place from a child's head down to its toes. They have managed to gain control of their arms and legs enough to produce forward movement. Then, once enough strength is developed, they pull themselves to the standing position, whether that is by hanging on to Daddy's leg or the living room sofa.

When your child begins to put some territory under his feet and really starts to move, it's the final stop on the march toward walking. This is called cruising. The story with which this chapter started gives you a vivid example of this stage and the monumental jump to actually walking without assistance.

OUR LITTLE EINSTEIN

Children are intent on learning about life. They are like little Einsteins working to understand their world. The development of fine and adaptive motor skills is critical to this process. While gross motor development is much more exciting to watch, fine and adaptive motor skills form the means by which children come to understand their world. Gross motor skills may get them a spot on the football team or cheerleading squad, but their fine motor skills and adaptive behavior will give them the information they need to develop those gross motor skills.

The first interaction with their environment occurs as they acquire the ability to grasp things. By six months of age, children develop the motor skills necessary to move their arms and hands in one motion closing their hands. Eventually, they manage to grab something, but it is purely by accident.

Innumerable parents and siblings have had their hair and other body parts pulled as a testimony to this developing ability. In spite of grabbing something, your baby doesn't have a clue about the connection between these two actions (moving the arms and grabbing an object). They may be grasping something, but they don't know they are holding it. There isn't that connection between their hands and their brains. That's why we have to forcibly pry their little fingers out of our hair or off our noses.

They will reach and grab for almost anything because they haven't learned what is solid and what isn't. That's why babies look like they are grabbing at thin air when they try to catch a ray of sunlight or something in the air that catches their attention.

To develop the understanding of what is to be grabbed and

what isn't, children will experiment with different objects. They will grab and shake, rattle, roll, bang, drop, and turn whatever they can get their hands on. They need to do this to gain a fuller understanding of the properties of objects—what is to be shaken for a certain sound and what is to be looked at. We can help them in their experiments by giving them new things to hold, look at, and mouth. You can shake something to get them interested and then sit back and watch the games begin.

For example, your six-month-old can probably grab a board book and shake it repeatedly. Before long, he will get bored because it really doesn't make any exciting sound. He will then turn his attention to a rattle or some other kind of noisemaker because of the exciting things it can do.

Over time, your baby will learn that the book can be shaken, but the best use of it is to look at the pictures with Mom or Dad. Our eighteen-month-old has become a real book lover. When anyone sits down, particularly her dad, she will ask expectantly, "Book?" and toddle over with one. This sequence of behavior is the result of long hours of looking at books together. She understands that books are to be looked at because of the process of grabbing and shaking the stuffing out of the book without success. She has found out through her experiments that there is something really fun about "reading" books.

At eight to ten months of age, babies begin to use their fingers to poke and prod objects. They use their index finger more than any other digit on their hand to point, poke, and check out the qualities of objects before touching them with their hands. The use of their index finger is an important precursor of the pincer grip that develops by twelve to fifteen months of age. Eventually, as their skill develops, they can grasp objects between their index finger and thumb instead of holding things in the palm. It is an important development in their ability to hold objects, examine them, and eventually use them as tools.

By age one, they have achieved enough facility with their grip to be able to drop objects into a box or can. A favorite toy of our kids was a coffee can with a square hole cut in the top of the plastic lid. We collected the metal tops of frozen orange juice cans. These could be dropped through the hole and made wonderful noises. Our kids' development of the pincer grip was easy to see. Initially, they would take off the lid of the can, discard it, and drop the can tops in (out of their palms) and take them out and do it all over. As they gained more accuracy, they would put the lid onto the can, hold the lid between the index finger and thumb, and drop the tops through the hole in the lid.

Using toys and other objects to accomplish tasks (like making noise) means a baby is using them as tools. This is an important development in your child's adaptive abilities. Your child will increasingly become aware that objects can be used for some purpose.

There are four important steps in this process vital to an understanding of objects and the world. The first step is *comparing* these objects. Toward the last three months of his first year, your child will hold an object in each hand, looking at each alternately as if to compare them. He will turn them over as if to figure out how they are different. Before long, he will begin to bang them together, put them in his mouth, drop them, throw them—whatever he can think of to manipulate these objects.

The next skill, *stacking,* is developed by about age one. Initially, most kids won't have the skill necessary to drop a block gently enough to maintain the stack. By fifteen months, he can probably stack two blocks, and by eighteen months he will move up to three blocks. Of course, as children are prone to do, they are not limited as we are by the "rules" of using just blocks to stack. They will try to stack just about anything small enough for them to pick up. This can include cubes, boxes, pots and pans, and their toys.

Have you ever noticed your little one gathering objects and putting them into a container? One day as I was preparing to study a book for my licensing examination, I discovered I couldn't find any of my highlighters. I looked all around my desk and my office at home. It had been picked clean of any writing utensil!

As I walked into the hallway, I was practically run down by a maniac two-year-old (Corrie) on her way to an important date with one of her dolls. In her grocery cart was every conceivable object she had the strength to pick up: all of my pens and pencils, canned vegetables, the dog's chewing toy, and other miscellaneous things. It was quite an event she had to attend, and of course, every object was necessary for the event to be a success. As annoying as this behavior might be, it is an important part of adaptive motor development. It is called *emptying and gathering.*

Nesting, the next adaptive skill developed, is when your child shows the insatiable desire to place things inside each other. As they experiment with this property of objects, they learn about size and the concept of inside and outside. A toy that will give your child hours of enjoyment is the nesting toy produced by most toy manufacturers in various forms. These toys not only give your child the opportunity to nest things together but also allow him to stack the same cups. Another fun activity is being turned loose on pots and pans. They are great items to nest together and are fun noisemakers, too.

The last step in adaptive behavior development is learning to use fingers to manipulate objects. A practical example of this behavior is how children manipulate the objects on their "busy box." Younger children will swipe at and hit their busy boxes to produce enough sounds to make them interesting. As your child gains strength and agility, he will be able to manipulate these items more effectively, making more enjoyable sounds.

The process of developing fine motor skills and adaptive behavior is involved. It takes time and effort. Thankfully, our kids have no lack of either one. Left to their own devices, they will do quite well in developing these skills. Yet, as with any other skill, direction is still needed. We need to be the ones who provide them the laboratory in which to work and give them direction to develop to their fullest potential.

LET'S GET PHYSICAL

Parents can encourage a child's potential motor skills by providing stimulation and encouragement. The stimulation needs to be as varied as you can make it. You won't need to spend a lot of money to help your child in this area. Simply focus on exercising his large and small muscle groups. One parent put it this way: "I always found that my children's best jungle gym was my own body. By carrying your baby in different positions, for example, in the football hold (his head in your palm, his body extended along your forearm), or in a front pack or backpack—you will enable him to see and absorb the world from many different perspectives."[2]

Stephen J. Langendorfer, Ph.D., associate professor of physical education and motor development at Kent State University in Ohio, encourages parents to "dance with their kids, get down on the floor and roll around or wrestle with them, take walks and play ball together. Lots of rough-and-tumble play is good for children."[3]

One tradition in our family is for my girls and me to "play wrestle." It begins when I lie down on the floor and they climb on for a "ride." This ride turns into a wrestling match when I get one down and tickle her, while another climbs all over me to try to stop me from "hurting" her sister. Sometimes I pick one up, hold her upside down, and gently lay her back down. Inevitably, the noise level reaches near bedlam proportions and someone cries uncle. This play not only exercises their little bodies but it gives them sensory information about their bodies in space. This kind of play helps them develop posture and balance, and confidence in their ability to control their bodies.

Parents can also create opportunities for their kids to develop hand-eye coordination much like the activity my girls and I share. Research suggests that babies who have been raised in traditional, residential nurseries with few toys and not much adult attention, and have spent hours in their cribs with nothing to do, are slow in learning to reach out and grab things. The moment they are given attention and interesting things to look at and handle, their hand-eye coordination develops quickly.[4]

Hand-eye coordination is as vital during the first six months of life as crawling and walking during the second six months. It provides the basis for other coordinated activities that inevitably involve the eyes and limbs, such as catching a ball and reaching for things. Here are a few ideas to encourage this:

- Routinely hold objects in front of your child to reach for and grasp. These can be anything you are holding at the moment.

- Put your child in a baby backpack and go for a walk. This gives him opportunity to hold his head up to look around and touch leaves and other items of interest.

- Get down on the floor with your child and roll him over gently. Each time, try to engage his eyes as you come into his view. This will give him practice finding you with his eyes, establishing a focus point after turning over, and enjoying the movement of his body.

- Put on some music and, while holding hands, help your child "dance" to the music. Again, this is great fun and helps him enjoy the movement of his body.

- If you have a wagon, take your little one for a ride. If he can sit up, he will use his hands to balance himself. The movement of the wagon over bumps and other obstacles will give his muscles practice at maintaining his posture with different positions.

While physical activities are important, you can't always be around to interact and play with your child. Toys can provide children with the opportunity to play independently and continue to develop their motor skills. Many toys allow you to participate with your child. When you can't be there, they allow you some independence while your child plays alone. The following toys are categorized by age range:

SIX MONTHS TO ONE YEAR

Books. What do books have to do with motor development? The board book's fat, stiff pages help develop fine motor skills because of the relative accuracy needed to turn the pages.

Activity centers. These centers, otherwise known as "busy boxes," provide children with various activities they can engage in, from turning a telephone-type dial to moving objects across the board and other ways of making noises. In spite of their name, these "busy boxes" are usually flat boards that have a variety of things children can do.

The activity center our children have includes a mirror, two figures at the bottom that move back and forth, a bulb to push and make a bell ring, a telephone dial, and a spinning dial with primary colors on it. It has straps that allow it to be attached to their bed rails and hang over the side so they can play with it in bed. With increasing maturation and development of fine motor skills, your child will be able to do these activities more effectively.

Balls and push toys. These are toys that also develop hand-eye coordination, by providing opportunities to practice kicking and catching the ball, and develop balance, by letting your child hang on to the bar or handle of the push toy.

Nesting toys. Many toy companies combine these nesting toys with stacking toys. Fisher-Price makes one set of toys that can be nested when placed together and can also be turned over and stacked to build a tower. These toys are important because of the fine motor development they facilitate (hand-eye coordination), as well as encouraging your child's understanding of colors, shapes, sizes, and numbers.

Stacking toys. Typically, these have a rocker base with a centrally placed rod. Soft rings can then be placed on this rod in decreasing sizes. Initially, your little one may be more interested in chewing on the rings. Eventually, he will become more interested in stacking them, at first in random order, later in the appropriate sequence.

Blocks. Even if your child seems too young or uninterested, get these now to help your child get used to playing with them. They will be used throughout his playing days. They help in motor development by encouraging hand-eye coordination and comprehension of the concepts of under, over, in, out, differential sizes, and colors. They also provide hours of stacking fun. When you play blocks with your kids, you can model for them building things, making "roads" by putting the blocks end to end, or anything else you can think of. Some of the fun your little one will have with you is destroying whatever you make!

As your child matures, you can encourage building things and understanding what he is doing by talking your way through a building project. For example, "Let's build a tower. First, I'll put this block here, and this one on top of it."

Walking toys. These toys generally have a chest-high handle or bar attached to a stable base with wheels and can be pushed around the room. They are great assistance in further developing their walking skills and other gross motor movements.

While these toys are oriented toward self-play, never forget to involve yourself in your child's play times. Not only is it a fun relationship time but it will give you the opportunity to expand the ways your child plays with toys.

My family loves to chide me about how I like to play Duplos more than my kids. On the other hand (and in my defense), one of my kids who watched me build things with rapt attention now loves to create her own little town and buildings.

ONE YEAR TO TWO YEARS OLD

Slides, riding toys, and swings. These items provide opportunities for your child to develop gross motor skills: walking, running, climbing, coordination. Riding toys are also helpful in exercising legs, and they help kids learn to ambulate more effectively than walking.

When you first put children on a riding toy, they may not catch on immediately to the idea and may even move backward rather than forward. Be patient. They will get the hang of it and move on to bigger things. In the same way, swings encourage coordination, giving your child sensory information regarding his body in space and different perspectives of the world.

Sand toys and water toys. Both of these kinds of toys give valuable sensory feedback. Playing in sand or water helps develop fine motor coordination and offers information for a child's cognitive development. You don't have to go to the local toy store to find these toys. There are few toys, other than ones that need to stay dry, that can't be used as a sand or water toy. Practically any object in your home used to measure liquids or other materials is especially useful as a sand or water toy. Of course, your local toy store will have small hand rakes, shovels, sieves, and various other toys that can be used in a sand box or play pool.

Shape sorters. These toys are usually shaped like a box with holes so that various shaped blocks can be placed through the holes. They are valuable for fine motor coordination and further cognitive development related to shapes, sizes, and colors. You can start your child very early with these toys. He doesn't have to be able to manipulate the blocks. You can move the shape sorter to the appropriate hole for him to put the block inside. Children are fascinated by this activity and before long will be doing it themselves as they gain better motor coordination and an understanding of shapes.

Dolls and other "housekeeping" toys. These toys enable your child to imitate you in your housekeeping activities. By the end of his second year, your little one will enjoy pretending to vacuum the carpet, wash the dishes, and perform other activities he has seen you do. The various toy companies produce toys for domestic play—plates, cups, and other housekeeping items. These toys apply equally to boys and girls. Pretend play extends to dolls for boys and girls as well. Children learn a lot about social relationships and interaction through this beginning stage of pretend play with their dolls.

Materials for playing dress-up. The best source of such clothes is garage sales. All types of clothes will do—hats, dresses, shoes, pants, and coats. This clothing can be adapted for your child to wear. It doesn't need to fit particularly well; putting on "big people" clothes is what makes it so fun.

Boys and girls alike enjoy playing grown-up. Of course, some clothes you have need to be men's clothing so that you can give your little boy an opportunity to imitate his daddy. Our girls have enjoyed visiting their grandmother's house because they can go downstairs, put on the play clothes, and play for hours as shopkeepers, princesses, and other characters. Parents can encourage this by asking the kids to put on a play.

One activity our girls have played with the next-door neighbors (who include a little boy) is playing "spy games." They sneak around the house wearing wide-brimmed hats "looking for clues," trying not to be seen by the "bad guys" (usually the unwitting parents) and carrying note pads for recording their clues.

Balls, frisbees, and other items to throw. These toys are self-explanatory. They develop gross motor skills and invite rolling, throwing, and kicking.

With the introduction of toys comes the risk of injury. Of course, this concern extends throughout childhood rather than being confined to this period. An estimated 130,000 toy-related injuries occur each year.[5] The sad thing is that most of the injuries are preventable. The more work we do as parents and caregivers to make sure our children's toys are safe and their use is supervised properly, the less likely an injury is to occur. We must take nothing for granted. Of course, our children do not have the life experiences necessary to ensure their safety. There will be no other time in their lives that we have more control over their physical environment. Because of this, we need to be conscientious in examining and testing out the toys we buy and give to them.

One valuable resource for information on toy safety is the Consumer Products Safety Commission. This governmental agency produces pamphlets and publications about a variety of products on the market. In addition, they have designed a no-choke testing tube that allows you to figure out if objects are small enough to pass through your child's esophagus. If the object can pass through this tube, it will be unsafe for use by your child. For more information about this item write:

> Toys to Grow On
> Department of Safe Toys
> P.O. Box 17
> Long Beach, CA 90801

ONE LAST NOTE

We must strive to encourage our children in both their gross motor skills and their fine and adaptive motor skills. Many parents focus on gross motor skills because progress is more visible and exciting. Some children thrive on the attention provided by their parents' focus on their physical capabilities. I'm not sure which provides children more incentive—the attention given by their parents, or the ease with which they find they can do things physically.

I hope you have concluded that your child needs varied and richly changing environments. I don't need to remind parents that nothing will replace walks, trips to the park, or bicycle outings, even if it is riding in a safety seat. These activities not only develop motor skills but provide valuable opportunities for interpersonal interaction between us and our children.

Our kids will benefit from an array of wide-ranging experiences and become people who have an unquenchable desire to find out more and develop a love of learning. These results may be not only physical but emotional, cognitive, and social. Remember, the work you do in any single area of your child's development will benefit all the other areas.

Chapter Five

Why, Mommy, Why?

One day I sat with our eighteen-month-old, Abby, playing with her shape-sorter. As she picked up each piece to put inside the box, she would first rotate it in her hands and look at it. It was almost as if she were sizing it up to see just what this thing was. Then, most methodically, she would attempt to push it into a hole, but it didn't fit. She would try it again, this time a little harder.

The next step in this developing drama was for her to let out a frustrated whine while she looked at me for help. I then turned the box over to the right side where the hole was and waited to see what she would do. On cue (we had done this routine before), she would then begin to push her cylinder into a hole for a rectangle. No good, that didn't work. She then tried the hole for a triangle—no good, that didn't work either. Finally, she tried the hole for the cylinder. Success! She was absolutely ecstatic. Her eyes lit up like little Christmas tree lights, and she looked up at me for the appropriate surprise-joy-enthusiasm-approval response to match her own pride of accomplishment.

But that wasn't the end of this experiment. She started banging on the top of the box with her little fist, making it painfully clear that she wanted to take out what had gone into this box. We dutifully emptied the contents of the box and started all over just as if we had never done it before.

Abby was exhibiting the hallmark of this stage of mental development: trial-and-error reasoning. As our children grow from infancy into toddlerhood, they increasingly become little scientists. They have an unquenchable curiosity about their world and how it works. This curiosity allows them to make mental pictures of what makes the world tick and what they can do to control it to get what they want.

Mental development is the integration of many different areas—motor, language, emotional, and social growth. The obvious reason for this is that mental development, by definition, is the integration of the information received by the senses. This information is put together to produce a picture of the world that allows us to interact with it effectively.

As you delve into your child's world of learning, remember that there is never a time when children are not learning. Everything that happens and the actions they perform are grist for their mental mills. Children are forming ideas and concepts about the world, and they continue to test these ideas to see if they hold true.

This may sound much more complex than it appears as you watch children do their "baby work." God has created us (little ones included) so that we effortlessly and automatically test out our hunches and discover more about our environment. Children's curiosity depends on that innate inheritance to know and control their world. I'm sure you have had more than enough painful experiences of just how true this is—like the times your little one imitates you at your worst moments. Children are truly, and for a long time, sponges who soak up their world and the people around them.

UNDERSTAND HOW THEY THINK

It was once thought that infants came into the world as a *tabula rasa*. In other words, a "blank slate" on which their experiences and other influences were written. (As a matter of fact, at one time infants were thought to be blind.[1]) New, exciting research suggests otherwise.

For example, one indicator of mental activity is the phenomenon of habituation. To understand this, think about the last time you showed your little one a toy or looked at a book. How long was his attention span? Let's say you put the book away. Then, when he came back to you, you pulled it out again. What does he do? More than likely, with each exposure to the book, his attention becomes shorter and shorter. This is habituation, the process by which we grow bored with something after repeated exposure to it. We must remember something before we can become bored by it.

We see this activity in infants. If a brightly colored picture with strong contrasts is shown to infants several times in a row, the babies will pay less and less attention to it each time. This suggests that they remember seeing it before and are growing bored with it. If you were to present a different picture to the babies, you would find them attentive again. Put these two aspects together and you can conclude that infants can discriminate between the two pictures not only on the basis of their features but also because they have seen one of them before.

Considering this research, we dare not underestimate the ability of infants to sense their world, and just how thrilling it is for them. One author put it this way:

> In the course of the initial half year or so, before they become capable of getting about on their own, babies soak up everything they can from their immediate surroundings with their ever-improving perceptual skills. But this is far from a passive and piecemeal process—it is an active and constant adventure. Each and every thing they are exposed to is a thrilling treasure to be explored and investigated fully with their eyes, ears, mouths, noses, and fingers. Simple items that you and I may hardly notice and take for granted because we have become familiar with them over a lifetime represent a whole world of wonder for the uninitiated and insatiably curious infants.[2]

A child's first year of life is, for the most part, focused on learning from the senses. The information they receive during this time is gained by trial and error instead of resulting from any planned behavior. Although their behavior is governed by reflexes, they are gaining important information about their environment that will provide the foundation necessary for increasingly purposeful behavior. At the same time, there is no yesterday, there is no tomorrow; there is only now. Whatever children receive right now is important and is to be enjoyed or rejected.

This suggests where parents should concentrate their efforts—variety for their baby's senses. Virtually anything you can hold in your hand can become something for your little one to see and experience. One of the most fascinating objects for our youngest daughter is the TV remote. It is black with brightly colored buttons. She thinks it's cool to see the remote and squeals with delight when it moves. It doesn't have to be anything dramatic or expensive. Everything is new in her mind; everything is novel.

Try to expose your child to as many sensory experiences as you can. Nothing in your immediate environment is immune from being exciting and novel to your little one. You will want to be alert to things that will stimulate not only their vision but their tactile senses, their hearing, and their taste.

As we mentioned in chapter 2, a truly pivotal point in the history of our understanding of children came when Jean Piaget began his study of children. His theory of cognitive development, published in 1952, was the result of years of unstructured observation of children, including his own three kids. His theory explains how a child learns about the objects and people around him, how to group objects, about cause and effect, and how he forms expectations of objects and events.[3]

According to Piaget, there are two inborn attributes that facilitate intellectual development. The first is *organization*. Organization occurs as the individual builds upon innate abilities such as seeing, hearing, and tasting, and uses the information gained from these abilities to build a more sophisticated understanding of the world. For example, when a child sees you ring a bell on his busy box, he has no idea that the ringing sound and the bell are connected. With time and experience, he will construct the "organization" in his mind that when you hit the bell a sound will result. He accurately connects the two events into a rudimentary understanding of cause and effect.

Notice the progression of understanding in the connection between hitting a bell and the sound of ringing: both sight and hearing are used (innate abilities) and then combined to arrive at a separate conclusion of cause and effect. One way this raw information is organized is through *assimilation*—taking new information and incorporating it into an already existing structure of understanding. If your little one were to go to his grandparents' house, and Grandma had a bell that rang when the timer went off, he could then take that new information and fit it into his already existing understanding of bells.

The other process by which organization is achieved is called *adaptation*. Adaptation occurs when your child changes his existing understanding of the world to incorporate new information. If your child were to strike the bell on his busy box with the rattle in his hand, he would find out that the bell could be rung in more ways than by the means provided in the busy box. This is adaptation. He adapts his understanding of how the bell is rung. Organization and adaptation allow him to adjust his understanding of the world around him, and his understanding becomes more sophisticated.

Piaget theorized that intellectual development goes through a series of stages. At each stage, children do not copy what they encounter but actively construct reality out of their experiences. These constructions are progressive approximations to adult reality and don't coincide with the adult vision of the world. Therefore, it is safe to say that both the content and form of children's thinking changes with age.[4]

From birth to approximately two years of age, the infant is concerned with constructing a world of permanent objects. In other words, he has no idea that objects and people exist when he cannot see, hear, feel, taste, or smell them. His rattle or teddy bear ceases to exist in his mind the moment he loses sight of it. These objects and people are not perceived as distinct entities by children. Instead, according to Piaget, children have to construct an understanding of these objects' permanence. The only way they gain this understanding is by acting upon them—pushing, banging, touching, dropping, and grabbing are among the actions typically taken by children. This aspect of their intellectual development is important to remember as we explore how to guide their natural curiosity. Children are "doers" at this stage of development and will need direction that builds upon this aspect of their learning.

GUIDING THEIR NORMAL CURIOSITY

When you consider how to help your children develop their intellectual skills to their greatest potential, remember two critical points. First, intellectual development is intricately related to the other areas of development we have reviewed. Intellectual development is dependent on information coming in from a variety of sources—hearing, sight, taste, touch, physical movements with large and small muscle groups, and social interactions. All these areas are vital to intellectual development because children are continually constructing and adapting to their world. Without this feedback, kids couldn't accomplish this critical process.

What this means for parents is that we have to work to give our children as many different experiences as we can—playing in water, watching the rainbow of colors reflected through a piece of crystal, playing with different materials (clay, sand, painting, coloring), talking to them as we do different things with them (changing diapers, taking a bath, watching siblings doing different activities).

Second, we must consider what it is we are *really* attempting to accomplish by encouraging our child's intellectual potential. Is it for you or for him? Were you so frustrated in your own process of growing up and achieving intellectual recognition that you vowed to save your child from experiencing the same thing? I know this is an extremely difficult question to answer honestly. But we must confront our motives honestly if we are to help our children develop their potential effectively. By not looking honestly at our motives, we will fall into a pattern of pressuring our children that will only result in disaster.

We all want to be convinced that our efforts to help our children are for their own good. All too often, though, we must admit that it is something inside us we are trying to correct or avoid by encouraging our children to achieve or overachieve. If so, you are likely to put undue pressure in this area and hamper your efforts to encourage and facilitate your child's development.

Jerry was such a parent. From the time his daughter began to sing, he could tell she was destined for greatness. She could carry a tune very early, and he dreamed how wonderful it would be to see her succeed in an area he couldn't. His own dreams had been dashed by a father who would simply not hear of his son singing in front of a "bunch of people." Singing was for women, he was told innumerable times. That didn't matter to Jerry. He loved to sing, but it went unnoticed and unencouraged.

When he saw his daughter's potential, his heart leapt for joy. He spent hours and hours with her singing and encouraging her with new songs and more music. On the surface, it all looked quite positive and helpful. But somewhere along the way something went wrong. At some point Jerry crossed the line between encouraging and demanding.

As any kid is prone to do, Jerry's daughter got tired of the intensity. She just wanted to play and have fun with the other kids. At this, Jerry got increasingly irritable and angry with his daughter. She had talent, and she had to use it. It was his job to see that her talent wasn't wasted like his own. The problem was that she recognized the fact that the achievement in this area wasn't for her, it was for her dad, and she rebelled.

It is dangerously easy to cross the line between encouraging our children's natural curiosity and potential and demanding such achievement. Your kids will be very aware of whom their achievement is for. The motivation to please you may help them for a while, but it will surely run out because the motivation is coming from outside them—namely from you. The really difficult thing is to find the balance between encouraging and pushing them.

We all need someone in our lives, maybe another parent we respect whose kids are out of the house, to provide us with perspective. We are simply too close to assess the situation ourselves. Here are a few questions to help you examine this area:

- Do you get mad when your child doesn't do as well as you know he can?

- What happens when he tells you he doesn't want to do the thing you know he can do?

- Does your child seem to be losing interest in an area you think he *should* be able to do?

- Do you seem to be investing more energy into an activity than your child is investing?

The critical issue in answering these questions is the intensity of your emotions when your expectations are not being met. That is the hard part about balance. It takes a lot of energy to figure out where we are in relation to what we want for our kids. Do we want their eventual independence and adjustment as people, or do we want them to achieve to make us look good?

Don't get me wrong, I am not saying take a laissez-faire attitude with your child's development. I'm saying that if we're honest about our true motives for pressuring our kids into achievement, we can do what is necessary to guard against the natural link between achievement and worth that our children make all too easily.

Make this an ongoing topic of discussion with your spouse so you can rein yourself in or your spouse can help you keep your expectations and personal issues out of evaluating your child's progress.

If your child isn't walking when he "should," and you translate that into a reflection on your parenting, you are sure to have some rather disturbing feelings about being a failure.

That's what happened to Jerry. His daughter wasn't following his agenda and he got increasingly angry. If Jerry had been discussing his feelings with someone and keeping his expectations in check, he would have been able to give achievement back to his daughter. He would have been able to "follow" her lead in her motivation toward singing, rather than demanding that she accomplish according to his standards.

The hallmark of encouraging our children is the ability to see the potential that is there and to help our children see it too. Then we can work together to develop it and enjoy the process along the way.

When our children are little, the true nature of their potential lies hidden for some time. In fact, when they begin life, they are all potential; they show little in terms of realized achievement. As they grow and achieve, we should always check ourselves to make sure we are encouraging them and not demanding achievement to satisfy our goals.

WATCH THOSE EXPECTATIONS

Our expectations are critical in facilitating the development of our children. That is one reason each chapter in this book includes an overview of developmental expectations. They have been included so you can adjust your expectations to what your child can do at any given level of growth.

There are times, in spite of how hard we work to adjust our expectations, that we still get sidetracked by our frustration over how "slow" our child's development is going. To keep our expectations under control, we have to remember that development is not a race, it is a process. We can make that process more exciting and exhilarating for our children, but we are probably not going to hurry the process by the things we do. Most children end in pretty much the same place at roughly the same time, although they may take separate routes and proceed at varying paces along the way.

When we hang on to our expectations so rigidly that it spills over into our relationship with our kids, they are perceptive enough to figure out that something about them is distressing Mom or Dad. The problem is, children don't have the capacity to separate their worth from how we feel about them. Therefore, the "logical" conclusion for them to make is that they are doing something wrong, or worse yet, something about them is wrong.

One author described expectations for developmental progress this way:

> Established milestones can provide a general picture of "typical" development during infancy and toddlerhood, but they can't provide a precise blueprint for the progress of any particular child. Although books, articles, and charts often may describe it in a concise and organized manner, the fact of the matter is that early development is never a neat and orderly affair; and while parents may want to compare his progress to that of other children and standard norms from time to time, they should never forget to appreciate and enjoy the special individuality demonstrated by their own child.[5]

Our expectations can often produce some wild ideas about how to facilitate our children's learning. These ideas have produced some very passionate parents as they strive to raise the "superkid." Nancy and Tom Biracree, in their book *The Parents' Book of Facts,* present the results of an exhaustive search of the literature regarding various early learning approaches to accelerate intellectual development. They came to three conclusions:

- No study has yet proven that accelerated or intensive preschool learning significantly improved the intellectual potential of middle-class children.

- Recent research into the early childhood experiences of unusually talented adults has revealed that their early childhood environments were exceptionally supportive and enriched. These environments included adults' reading to them and reading with them, trips to the park and museums, accessibility to various activities that encouraged creativity and exploration, and an opportunistic approach to learning or teaching about anything they and their parents experienced together.

- There's growing evidence that some kinds of accelerated or intensive preschool learning can cause moderate to severe developmental problems at some point between infancy and the teenage years. One common problem found by researchers is greatly increased stress that causes behavioral and emotional problems.[6]

Developmental psychologist David Elkind addresses this area of childhood stress in his book *The Hurried Child*. He proposes that in helping our children excel and achieve, we are hurrying them. We expect them to do things before they are ready emotionally, intellectually, and physically. Such things that children have been asked to deal with include caring and accepting parenting responsibility for other siblings, traveling alone, enduring the breakup of their families by divorce and separation, becoming "latchkey" kids, and the shifting of academic expectations even down to kindergarten. The result of such hurrying is that they are reaping a disastrous harvest of stress beyond their years and experience.[7]

Again, circumstances may place us in some difficult situations with our kids, and at times we may have to ask them to do things beyond their age. It is the "big picture" here that we're focusing on. At the same time, we have to be committed to allowing them to grow up before expecting them to do things that are not appropriate to their age.

VARIETY IS THE GOAL

You're probably asking by this point, "How do I keep that balance?" The answer is to give your child a variety of toys, stimulating activities, and experiences. If you can keep these aspects of their environment fresh and new, you will more than likely maintain balance in your approach to their learning.

This variety can include sophisticated toys and the simple objects in your house. Some parents have gotten so taken with enriching their child's learning environment that if you looked in the crib it would look like control central for NASA! It's incredible how many kids seem to thrive on the simplest toys rather than ones with all the bells and whistles. Here are some examples of simple, household playthings:

A good set of pans will keep your little one busy for a long time. It's fun for kids to take them out and put them back into the cupboard. Pans are good for stimulating a variety of senses—hearing (banging them together), motor coordination (the use of limbs to get them in and out of the cupboard), intellectual development of understanding size, weight, and shape (the nesting capabilities of some sets of pans). Remember, everything is a learning activity for your little one.

A batch of dough will also provide hours of fun with an inexpensive set of cookie cutters and other items out of your utensils drawer. This provides kids with a whole array of sensory information. They have to use their hands and fingers to fashion things as simple as the ever-popular "snake." Their sense of touch is stimulated by feeling and manipulating the dough. Their imagination is kindled in making various objects to proudly display.

Another fun activity is *playing in the bathtub*. When they are very small that may mean lying on their backs and splashing with their legs and hands. This stimulates their sense of touch with the sensation of water and hearing as they listen to the resulting noises.

Babies spend very little time undressed, and playing in the bathtub helps them get used to their bodies. As they grow, let them sit in the tub with something to prop them up (you holding them up, or you can buy a three-legged ring that attaches to the tub bottom with suction cups and helps them stay upright). Never leave your child alone even with this kind of prop. Play with things that float, things they can pour from (measuring cups from the kitchen). An ordinary kitchen baster filled with water is a great squirter.

These are just a sampling of the things you can use to help kids develop intellectually. Use your imagination as you work around the house and see things to play with that would provide a slightly different experience than your child has previously had. The list of toys given in the chapters on motor development and the newborn are equally applicable.

Don't forget to put some toys away periodically, and emphasize others your child hasn't played with for a while. Our kids, just like us, get bored with the same playthings every day. Rotating play toys and materials continues to provide variety, even if it means using something that's been around the house for a while.

I CAN'T DO WITHOUT MY PLAY!

Children never stop learning. They don't need structured times of learning. Yet for many parents, play represents a "waste of time." We must realize that play and learning go hand in hand. One can't happen without the other, particularly during the time our kids are growing.

Play is more than fun for your child. It is truly kid "work." Play provides children with the freedom to explore, test, and learn new things about their ever-expanding world. At this age range (birth to two years), play is learning. It is finding things out, and using the senses in all sorts of ways. This will invariably develop mental skills and understanding.

Playing with your little one is also an opportunity to teach him new things about you, about his own body, and about his world. The game of "Where is your (insert a body part)?" is an example of one such teaching tool. It begins the process of knowing his body and using language to identify himself.

Another simple game is "Peek-a-boo." The beauty of this game is that it can be played for quite some time with a multitude of variations. You can begin by covering his face with a blanket for a moment, and say, "Where is (his name)?" Then uncover his face and say "Peek-a-boo!" You can reverse it to say, "Where is Daddy?" As they grow, they can then do it themselves by putting the blanket over their own heads or over your face. This game begins to give them the opportunity to see they are separate from us, and that we exist even if they don't see us.

A favorite in our home is "How big is (child's name)?" When our kids were little (we started them at around four months of age) we would ask the question and then raise their hands above their heads. This was a great interactive game, tapping into not only language and social development but also gross motor development as we raised their hands above their heads. As they grew up, they began to get the hang of the game. As their language increased, they lifted their own hands above their heads in response to the question. It was a fun game that gave us an idea of our kids' receptive language and gave them some exercise.

Here are four things you can do to make the most of your individual play time with your child:

Provide planned play times. This can be something as simple as sitting and playing with the shapesorter like I did with my daughter, or more elaborate activities like going to a children's museum to explore the different exhibits there.

One parent I talked to would periodically sit with her toddler and make things with the play dough. The project was to make things for Daddy. When Dad got home, these would be proudly displayed on the table during dinner for his oohs and aahs.

You can also follow your little one's lead. If you see him or her in the sandbox, go out, sit down, and watch. Then start playing. Begin to make your own creation while talking about what you are doing. Your child's curiosity will get the best of him, and he'll want to get involved somehow, even if it is by waiting for you to finish so that he can knock it down!

This suggestion is a challenge when you have more than one child. If you are in that situation, vary the activities with each kid. As I mentioned earlier, I "play wrestle" with my girls, and then when we have completed that (usually when someone gets "hurt"), I will sit with my youngest and look at a book with her. The others can get their own books and look at them until the youngest goes to bed. That allows them some time to quiet down before bedtime, and allows me time to spend with Anne, my next-youngest daughter.

Adjust your play to your child's mood. One father told me that when he gets home all he has to do is listen. The decibel level tells him the state of affairs with his rambunctious little boys. He will then check with his wife and ask her what the boys need—sometimes they need to have some play time to run off some energy; other times, some quiet time to slow down. He acts accordingly.

If they are in a quieter mood, it may be time for a game of "Where is …?" or reading a book that has flip-out figures they can explore in your lap. As you can tell, this suggestion requires your understanding of where your child is emotionally. You and your spouse will probably need to work out some system by which you communicate with each other about what the kids need in terms of play.

Adapt your methods to the age of your playmate. You will need to slow your reactions and make them more dramatic when playing with a child two years old and younger. We're always having to remind our oldest daughter, Corrie, to slow down as she plays with her baby sister, Elizabeth. She attempts to play "Peek-a-boo" with her, but at a pace that is appropriate for an older child. Elizabeth must feel like she's in a whirlwind when her oldest sister whips the diaper from her face. Her poor eyes whirl from the intensity of activity!

Naturally, your child's perceptive abilities are not up to the speed of yours, so your voice will need more variation and enthusiasm for him to catch the drift of what you are doing. When you smile, your smile will need to be held longer to give them time to respond to what you are doing.

Adjust your games to your little one's personality. One of my daughters, Anne, is much more of a rough-and-tumble player than the other ones. It matches her personality. She is much more of an action kind of kid. She's always into something.

On the other hand, Corrie is much more placid in her personality, and on occasion may get into the rough-and-tumble mode, but often prefers quieter things—reading a book, coloring, playing with her dolls, and pretending with them. She, like many other kids, likes quieter games that aren't as physical.

Adapt to your children's personalities. To expect them to conform to your expectations of what is play ignores their individuality and uniqueness.

How do you remember all this? First, think of balance. Yeah, I know you're getting sick of hearing that word, right? That's OK. Balance provides us with a healthy tension to maintain our focus on encouraging our kid rather than producing a "superkid." We need to keep working on as many levels as we can—not all levels at once. We don't want to take a laissez-faire attitude; neither do we want to take an "I'm going to produce a genius" attitude. Where is the middle ground? It can be found in encouraging, supporting, and sometimes following your child's lead.

The second key is emphasizing the process over the production of certain abilities. Remind yourself that your child's development is not a race, it's a process. You are not trying to beat somebody in having your child walk, talk, and run before anyone else. If you adopt this approach you will do so at a grave price—usually your relationship with your child. We have to "work the process." In other words, we have to focus on enjoying their growing up, encouraging their exploration, and sharing their excitement of new things. If we devote ourselves to this process, the result will take care of itself.

Chapter Six

Relationship 101

The ability to relate to others well is crucial to getting our needs met and meeting the needs of others. As you lay the foundation for your little one's social and emotional development, it's important to realize the gravity of the undertaking. Our children may have all the intelligence in the world and yet be dunces when it comes to relating to people. They may excel physically but not be able to carry on a healthy relationship. A person's social skills and emotional health provide the backdrop for all other achievements.

The weight of this responsibility could overwhelm us if we forget that we're not parenting alone. We must rest on the knowledge that God has foreordained us as the parents of our children. There are no accidents in God's plans for us. Jeremiah 29:11 says, "'For I know the plans I have for you,' declares the Lord, 'plans to prosper you and not to harm you, plans to give you hope and a future.'" Even if we don't think we're doing such a good job as parents, or a child is particularly difficult, God will see that his plans for our children are completed. "Being confident of this, that he who began a good work in you will carry it on to completion until the day of Christ Jesus" (Phil 1:6).

We don't have to be perfect parents; we only have to be "good enough" parents. I've seen too many parents strive to be "the best" for their children and sabotage their efforts because they inevitably made mistakes. When we allow ourselves to be "good enough," we recognize our need for divine wisdom to raise our kids. This means that we can meet them at their level of need—comforting them when they hurt, empathizing with them in their disappointments, and encouraging them when they get discouraged.

We don't have to be perfect for every occasion. Our shortcomings (although we would never choose them) are often the instruments God uses to teach our kids important lessons about life. If we view our shortcomings and mistakes as normal and expected and see them as an opportunity to show our children a balanced view of the world and its difficulties, God will teach our children through us.

Children will also learn about themselves in the crucible of their families. They will learn about their emotions and appropriate ways to express them, depending on the family.

Within the family they will also learn their limitations. They will find out they aren't as powerful as they once thought. Neither is the world as safe as they once thought. Fortunately, there are bigger and more powerful people to get things done for them. Yet their drive for independence will motivate them to move farther and farther away from these significant people.

Finally, they will learn all about love—giving and receiving it. At first they will only be concerned about getting their physical needs met. As they grow in relating and bonding with the important people in their lives, they will come to find out how important it is to be loved and valued by another person.

As they interact with their family, they are forming ideas about what a "good" relationship is (as defined by their family relationships). They're also figuring out what to look for in the future, in their quest for intimacy, to duplicate this good relationship.

Our children cannot discern a truly healthy relationship. All they know is what they see, and they assume that the way things are in their family is the way things should be. This points out even more powerfully the importance of working to have healthy relationships in our families.

Social and emotional development is the cornerstone of healthy living, and it provides the backdrop that will either facilitate or hinder the other areas of your child's development.

To lay a foundation for your child's future social and emotional development, you will need a basic understanding of three concepts: bonding, social growth, and emotional development.

ARE YOU MY MOTHER?

Bonding, as we explored in chapter 2, has been called *attach-ment* by researchers who have looked closely into how we relate to one another. One figure prominent in explaining the process of attachment was a British psychiatrist named John Bowlby.

Bowlby proposed that the attachment made between humans derives from a need for security and safety. These needs develop early in life, are usually directed toward a few specific individuals, and endure throughout the remainder of life.[1] Forming attachments is normal, healthy behavior not only for children but for adults as well.

One day my daughter Abby and I ran errands that included a stop at a colleague's office. As we waited for him, she sat patiently— for a while. Before long, her curiosity got the best of her and she squiggled and squirmed off my lap. She looked around, torn between the novelty of this new place and the security of being with me.

As her familiarity with the room increased, she explored further and further away from me. She was even forward enough to venture near my friend and shoot him a smile to see his response. Being the friendly type, he responded appropriately, and the game was afoot. She quickly scurried back into my lap for protection and security. This lasted for only moments before she squirmed off my lap to take another adventurous jaunt into the "great un-known" to keep this fun game going.

This illustrates the concept of attachment. When children are "securely attached" to another person, they have the freedom to explore more of their world while knowing there is a secure base where they can return. The goal of the child's attachment behav-ior is to keep the emotional bond intact.

Mary Ainsworth, a student of Bowlby, further expanded his concepts to arrive at three separate categories of attachment behavior in infants based on their reactions to an unfamiliar situa-tion when their mothers left the room.[2]

One group of infants protested or cried on separation, but when their mother reentered the room, they greeted her with smiles and pleasure. The infants frequently held out their hands to be picked up. When they were picked up, they molded to their mothers' bodies. In spite of the separation, they were relatively easy to console. This group was called "securely attached."

The second group was called "anxiously" or "insecurely" attached. These children became terribly anxious and afraid when their mothers left, and they didn't attempt to explore their surroundings. They would cry profusely and sometimes uncontrollably. When mother returned, her baby would seek contact much like the securely attached infant but would simultaneously arch away from her angrily when she tried to soothe his frayed feelings.

The third group of babies was called "avoidant." This group of kids gave the impression they didn't need their mothers. They would often explore their surroundings without using their mothers as a base from which to work. Often they wouldn't even look back to make sure their mothers were there. When a mother left, her child acted as if nothing of concern had occurred. When mother returned, the child would snub or avoid her.

The upshot of this research points out that the responsive parent provides a secure base from which the infant can operate. It's important that the child know that his primary caregiver (whether mother or father) is steady, dependable, and consistently there for him. Armed with this understanding, the child is able to venture forth and explore his world without concern that Mom or Dad will be gone when he gets back. Lacking this understanding, he is insecure and his exploratory behavior is impeded.

Another key to healthy attachment is linked to a child's cognitive development. Understanding the concept of time is a developmental milestone during the first two years of life. How is this connected with attachment? Unless children have developed a sense of "now" and "later," they will not understand what it means for you to leave and return. As strange as this may sound, separation anxiety, which develops during the later part of the first two years of life, is a good indication of the strength of the emotional bond between parent and child.[3]

Not only is an understanding of time important, so is a child's ability to understand that you still exist in spite of the fact they can't see you. Children who haven't developed this cognitive ability (object permanence) believe that when they can't see you, you are truly gone. It's as if you've abandoned them never to return.

This is not to imply we should never leave our kids, but it's important to understand their intense reaction to our absence. It represents their best attempt to reestablish their emotional bond with us. Without our presence, they are incomplete and lack a sense of themselves. The important thing is to understand their anxiety, comfort them for a time, but eventually still leave. Over time, they will manage to connect with someone else to be comforted.

Maybe you're wondering why this is so important. Does something that occurs so early in a child's life really affect their future behavior? Yes. One study by Philip Shaver and Cindy Hazen explored the effects of a person's early bonding experiences with the quality of his or her romantic relationships later in life. In their study, Shaver and Hazen polled 620 readers of the *Rocky Mountain News* and 108 college freshmen, asking them about "the most important relationship they'd ever had, how they experience love, and how they think the course of romantic love goes for most people."[4]

These researchers used three categories to classify the responses. "Securely attached" people believed it was easy to get close to others, and they had no problem with mutual dependency in a relationship. Those who formed "avoidant" attachments agreed that they feel uneasy when people get too close, and they have trouble trusting and depending on others. The third group, called "anxious/ambivalent," included people who said they wanted a level of closeness many partners didn't seem willing to give, and they worried a lot about loved ones leaving them.

What these researchers found was that secure people had particularly happy, trusting, and friendly love relationships. Their romantic relationships tended to last the longest of all groups and ended in divorce the least often. The avoidant group reported a fear of intimacy, emotional highs and lows, and jealousy in their relationships. The anxious people reported an even higher frequency of emotional highs and lows and intense jealousy. They also indicated a desire to "unite" with their partners and to have their partner match the intensity of their feelings.[5]

Shaver suggested that "attachments formed in infancy don't *necessarily* (italics added) repeat themselves in adulthood. Parents may change their initial behavior toward their child, or a child might form a close, stable bond with another family member or friend. Some people may manage to work out the problems early relationships may have caused and establish better relationships as adults."[6]

In other words, don't despair if you see these tendencies in your child. No matter what your child's age, it's not too late to make some changes. One mom I had occasion to work with in counseling noticed the avoidant pattern in her son and herself. She directed her attention toward the people who could help her refute the irrationality of her fears, and she concentrated on staying closely involved with her son by doing things with him (playing, reading to him) and praying with him for God's protection and safety. This combination helped her make progress in both areas.

Sometimes it's necessary to seek advice from a Christian counselor who can help you identify these patterns and make changes so that your child can have a healthier relationship with you and others in the future.

WILL YOU BE MY FRIEND?

When I was completing my graduate training, I worked for a community mental health center. While there, I was involved in leading socialization groups for young children. They were composed of young (three- to five-year-old) children who came from underprivileged families where the parents were unable to meet their needs for social relationships. Many of these parents were terribly wounded from their own families and were incapable of emotionally bonding with their kids. These groups provided the kids with an environment that was safe enough to let them learn how to relate both to their peers and to adults.

I'll never forget one little girl whose only playmate at home was a puppy. When I drove her home, she would head back to the doghouse to find her playmate. Upon her approach, a little head would peer out from the darkness, ears perked up, head cocked to one side. She would then drop to her knees and begin whimpering and nuzzling her playmate for affection and attention. She had learned the rules of relating to a puppy, but she struggled to relate to people. This little girl was like the bird in the popular Dr. Seuss book *Are You My Mother?* She had searched for a friend to bond with, and the only one she found was a puppy. As sad as this story is, it points out that children need someone with whom to relate and will often find it wherever they can.

Socialization is the process of learning the rules of relating to other people. It is a lengthy process that many still struggle with at times—what to say when greeting someone, what to expect when someone gets angry, how to accept gifts from people, how to listen to others, what to say when you do something wrong, and so on. Not only do we need to learn the rules of relating but we need to learn to control our behavior to participate fully in society. In a sense, that is the twofold role the family plays in socialization—teaching both how to have healthy relationships with people and how to fulfill the role of a responsible person in a larger society.

For the most part, the first year of a child's life is consumed with relating and focusing on caregivers and interacting with them. Increasingly, caregivers are given a more central role in the child's understanding of himself in a social unit.

In the second year of life, parents still dominate the picture, but in a different way. They play a more instructive role in helping children learn how to control their behavior, fit into the social unit of the family, and learn to accept correction for bad behavior.

Two interrelated processes—modeling and imitation—dominate the picture as children awaken to the social world around them. Our children are always watching us to see how we handle life. Through this observation they begin to understand how to master their world. Naturally, children are strongly influenced by what they see. As the old saying goes, "Monkey see, monkey do." Modeling works by showing a person how to behave, and this influences their subsequent behavior.

Albert Bandura and his colleagues, in their now-famous studies on children's imitation of aggressive behavior, showed convincingly that what children see they attempt to do as a means of learning how to behave. In his research, children would watch on film a model (an adult) hit a "bobo" doll (the kind that when hit will return to an upright position) or sit quietly next to the doll. What the researchers found was that those children who had watched the aggressive model attacking the "bobo" doll were likely to do the same behavior as the model. Those who watched the model sit quietly would imitate that behavior. Although this is not a revelation to any parent, it did provide convincing proof of the effect modeling has on children's behavior.[7]

One way parents can help children learn appropriate social

behavior is by encouraging their kids to play dress-up. By dressing up, children take on a role modeled by the parents or other significant people. This kind of play provides a safe environment in which to learn the roles of relating and how to act in appropriate ways. It allows children to act out their own frightening or inappropriate feelings through the role of someone else.

Other benefits of such dressing-up games are learning to take turns (deciding who is going to be who in the drama they are developing), asking for help and helping one another (one child can't get a piece of clothing on and another one helps), and solving problems (working out the props for their play). It is a way to practice roles without worrying about mockery or being judged for behavior the child has never tried before.

THE FOUNDATION OF RELATING—TRUST

As we briefly explored in chapter 2, Erik Erikson explained emotional growth in terms of the challenges or conflicts an individual must resolve to be able to engage in healthy relationships. The first stage, trust versus mistrust, spanned the first twelve to eighteen months of life. This sense of trust is probably better characterized as a sense of the dependability of or confidence in the primary caregivers. In describing how the infant relates and counts on his caregivers, Erikson states that the child "has learned to rely on the sameness and continuity of the outer providers."[8]

To ensure the best results in helping a little one resolve conflict, a parent must provide consistency so the infant will know the parent will always be there. This means we won't have to be overly concerned with "spoiling" our little ones with attention (particularly during the first year of life). We can respond freely to their needs without "adultifying" their demandingness by attributing adult thoughts and motives to them.

The skill parents need to learn is the ability to respond to a child's needs and recognize them for what they are rather than interpreting them into some demanding or defiant behavior. The implication is: when they cry, we respond; when they laugh, we laugh with them; and when they struggle with the frustration of not being able to do what they want, we encourage them with soothing words of reassurance. As they grow and become more proficient in meeting their own needs, we won't need to jump at every whimper or cry. Maintaining an openness to responding when needed and not responding when they are capable of doing something for themselves is the key to helping our children develop a healthy level of independence appropriate to their age.

Erikson describes the task of parenting as "creating a sense of trust in (one's) children by that kind of administration which in its quality combines sensitive care of the baby's individual needs and a firm sense of personal trustworthiness."[9] In other words, our job as parents of children ages one to one-and-a-half is to be consistent in meeting the physical and emotional needs of our children. Through this consistency they can begin to trust the important people around them.

The latter half of the period we are examining in this section is when the second conflict or crisis of childhood occurs. It will extend through the third year of life. Erikson calls this the crisis of *autonomy versus shame and doubt.* Children enter this stage when they become more mobile. They are now confronted with the ability to move away from us as well as move back into closeness again.

As we have seen in the section on attachment, kids will use the parent as a secure base from which to explore their world. What Erikson adds to that picture is an understanding of the conflict that gets acted out before our eyes when our little one ventures away and then scurries back to the security of our lap. In doing so, children are developing the emotional fortitude to be independent. They are torn between the intense drive to be independent and the need to be secure and safe.

This crisis is best exemplified in the term "terrible twos." Children this age are fiercely independent, screaming to get away from you as if you had some deadly communicable disease. The next moment they cling to you as if they would die if you left them. A parent must learn to develop balance and flexibility during this stage of their child's emotional development. When children are ready to cuddle, do it freely without residual hurt feelings from being shunned by a two-year-old. When they are ready to run, let them run. It's hard to have such an openhanded approach, but if we are going to maintain any sense of sanity, we have to develop the ability to let go and let them do what they are driving to do—grow up and away.

This means that when two-year-olds flex their "independence muscles," it's time to capitalize on it and encourage them through our words and actions to do what they can for themselves. For example, most two-year-olds can feed themselves, drink from a cup with a spout, or look at a book by themselves. Encourage them to do these things.

On the other hand, when they are clinging and fragile, we must adjust our expectations. It's all part of the internal conflict our children are trying to resolve—being away and independent feels good; being close gives the child the security he needs. What results is a negativism and extreme vacillation between opposing styles of relating (dependence and independence) that can drive a parent crazy.

Our children must experiment with these extremes. Our job is to encourage the process and try to keep it heading in a healthy direction—toward a healthy interdependence, which means that when they feel needy they can ask for comfort, and when they feel independent they can ask for room to explore without fear of recrimination.

Erikson describes the implications of the resolution of this conflict best when he writes: "From a sense of self-control without loss of self-esteem comes a lasting sense of good will and pride; from a sense of loss of self-control and of foreign over-control comes a lasting propensity for doubt and shame."[10]

As parents, we are indispensable to our children's social and emotional development. We are not only the models for appropriate behavior, we are the instructors of the same. We are also our children's base of emotional security from which they can explore and interact with the world.

CRYING AND COMFORTING

As our children progress from birth to two years of age, the issue of crying and comforting looms ever larger. It is during these times that a child learns a great deal about parents and how consistent they will be in meeting the child's need for security. As the above section on attachment makes clear, the name of the game is consistency and compassion for the state of affairs of your little one's world.

The only language a six-month-old to one-year-old has is crying. Allowing a child to cry simply because he needs to learn to work it out for himself is both dangerous and speaks a deadly message. A child whose parents have this attitude will grow up believing that when you feel bad, you can't always depend on your parents (or other significant people) to be there for you.

Again, this is where flexibility comes into play. Our response has to be consistent within the context of our children's distress. If they are crying out of anger or frustration, then we need to allow them to cry. On the other hand, if the crying is in the midst of a temper tantrum, then maybe it's time for them to head to the nearest chair until they can quiet down.

The last suggestion applies only if a child has already shown the capacity to quiet himself. If that isn't true, then you may need to take your child to the chair or a quiet place and talk him through it ("I'm sorry you're so angry, but you will need to stop crying so that we can talk"). We need to accept where our children are emotionally and help them develop the skills necessary to handle their own emotions in a healthy way.

As they continue to grow and become more autonomous, the world is an alluring and curiosity-provoking place, but it is also unsure and unknown. They wonder when they venture away from us if we'll still be there when they return. When children are in distress, we have a powerful moment to teach them we will be there for them.

Consistency and acceptance are critical in helping children with their emotions. A child's emotions are no different than our own, except that children don't know how to control and manage their emotions.

Adults have the ability to neutralize an experience. For example, if I were looking forward to a long-awaited vacation and something arose to prevent it, I could deal with it by saying, "Oh well, there will be another opportunity to go. Besides, this needs my attention more than a vacation." Or I could minimize the impact of that emergency by saying, "I really didn't feel like going anyway." Whatever the means chosen, our intellectual abilities allow us to make the disappointment less poignant. This is simply not possible for a toddler.

Your little one is coping with intense emotions. What this means is that our response to such emotions should be compassion first and instruction second. Too many parents try to instruct their children at the worst possible times. We must meet their emotions with an emotional response, not with a teaching response. There will be plenty of time for instruction and training later.

I remember once when I had come home from a meeting, my eldest daughter, who was two or three at the time, came running in to meet me with tears streaming down her face. When I picked her up, I recognized that she was terrified.

"What happened, Cor?"

"The lions ate up a poor deer!" she sobbed.

"Oh my, that must have been scary. I'm sorry that it scared you so much. Let's go watch the rest of the movie together, OK?"

I didn't use the opportunity to instruct her in the ways of nature and how cruel it can be. I had the foresight (often rare) to see that I needed to match her emotions with a recognition of that emotion. It was only later, after she quieted down and could hear me that we talked about how "cruel" animals seem to be with each other, and what happened to make nature that way.

Acceptance of our children's emotions will not spoil them or encourage them to react to every unsettling experience. That is where balance comes in. We must strive to deal with their emotions in a caring and loving manner (remember you are modeling), and at the appropriate time help them think of other ways to deal with their feelings if necessary.

We need to validate our kids' feelings; let them know it's OK to feel the way they do. Helping them identify how they feel and talking about those feelings with them communicates the message "I hear you and accept what you feel." That is what I did for my daughter. She probably didn't recognize the fact that she was scared and mad about the lion, but by talking about it I helped expand her understanding of her feelings.

Another concern many parents have is that by "accepting" their child's feelings they are condoning them. Isn't that what we want to do? We may not want to condone the thinking that went into the emotional response, but we are going to have to wait for a better time to get to that. When someone accepts your feelings, they are accepting you. That is true of our children, too. Accepting their feelings accepts them. For this season of their lives, the emphasis has to be on comforting, not exhorting them to buck up.

Bedtime is probably the most trying time of the day for parents, since they tend to lose the most sleep over it. Children cry at bedtime because of the issues attached with being bonded with their parents and being separated from them. Their response is similar to when they are left for any other reason. They just don't understand they are not being abandoned to a dark room never to see us again.

Most pediatricians, psychologists, and mental health workers would agree that a "transitional object" is a good idea to facilitate the separation that sleeping forces upon our little ones. As the name implies, this object acts as a bridge between your constant presence and your absence. The object can comfort them back to sleep and help them develop the ability to comfort themselves. A transitional object can be a blanket, a stuffed toy, or any other item.

These three strategies can help you learn how to assure your children of your presence and consistency while encouraging them to look to themselves to provide the comfort necessary to get to sleep.

Develop a bedtime routine. For example, read to your child and rock him for a time. The actual elements aren't as important as the establishment of the routine. Over time, your child will begin to understand that when the routine starts it is time to get ready to go to sleep.

Use the same transitional object for sleep times, sick times, and other times associated with becoming quiet. This can begin shortly after birth. By doing so, your child will come to see it as a signal for going to sleep and will learn how to comfort himself.

Once your child is in bed, meet his crying with periodic assurances of your presence by going into his room, patting him on the back, and leaving again. You may have to lay him back down in bed and tuck him in as well. This process may need to be repeated until he finally goes to sleep.

LET'S GET SOCIAL!

Getting two one-year-olds together, or two toddlers together, is like putting a cat and dog in a very tiny space. Much like the children's story of the "Calico Cat and Gingham Dog," it looks like they are going to eat each other up. The exasperating thing is that even though you know your children need social contact to develop social skills, they have very little interest in learning such things. They have no understanding that they are only one person in a world of innumerable individuals. They don't understand the consequences of their behavior and that others have feelings too. It makes for slow going, to be sure.

It might help you relax to know that your toddler will probably not be ready to be a "good" playmate until his third birthday. Here are a few ideas that might give you some direction in getting your child used to social interaction.

- Be sure to arrange for your little one to have playmates. You will probably notice certain kids your child will have better success being around in terms of sharing toys and playing. This may be the child to invite over for more play time together. Even if your child is too young to be a cooperative playmate, he will still love being with other kids and will get to watch others play and learn by watching them.

- Be careful not to force social interaction between your child and other children. Give him time to warm up to the other kids and venture out on his own into the world of playing. Give your child a secure base from which to work and interact with others.

- Begin to teach him simple social skills like saying "Hello" when he sees his friends and "Thank you" when they do something nice for him. When they are given something by someone else, begin by modeling "Thank you" for them. Then as they grow and their language skills expand, ask, "What do you say?" after they receive something to prompt them to say "Thank you."

- Initiate simple lessons on sharing. Start by teaching them about the concept of ownership. When they grab something from another child, take it and say, "No, this is Johnny's toy; let's find something else to play with." This is the beginning of learning about boundaries.

- Don't forget to teach by example. Be a good model yourself. The way you greet your little one, show concern, talk with him, share, and handle your own angry impulses will most certainly influence the way he will act toward other children.

BOUNDARIES AND EMOTIONS

Early in our children's development, there is no real need to be concerned about emotions and boundaries. Boundaries are the area where your responsibilities end and where another person's begin. It is the space in which you are responsible and includes your emotions, your thoughts, and your behavior. There aren't any personal boundaries between parent and child for some time, since children need their parents to provide them with the security to deal with their world. Most of the responsibility for them rests with the parents. Therefore, boundaries aren't really an issue in the early stages of growth.

As children become more independent and responsible for themselves, the issue becomes much more important. How they behave and the choices they make will tax your understanding of your worth as a person.

During the process of attaching and bonding with our kids, we quite easily "become one" with our children, involving a certain amount of fusion between us and them. Therefore, when they act out or act poorly toward others, it is as if we have committed the blunder. The boundaries between our children and ourselves get blurry. Their poor behavior is our poor behavior, and we act accordingly—ashamed and embarrassed. As a child moves beyond his first year of life and into his second and third, this will be particularly true.

How do we allow our children, even relatively young ones (eighteen months and older), to express their emotions without taking them on as our own? This is a critical issue that affects the future of your relationship with your children in profound ways.

The most telling example is how we choose to deal with the negativism of the "terrible twos." If your little one pushes the limits with you, and you curtail his behavior either through a swift swat to his bottom or a spank to his hands, how do you feel after it's all over? Do you feel guilty for making him cry? Does the sound of his crying get to you so much that you have to leave? Do you make yourself available for comforting and restoration after the discipline? These questions begin to address boundaries with your little one. How you respond to this kind of discipline situation reveals your ability to separate your emotions from your child's. When you are able to comfort him with freedom and compassion after discipline, you communicate three important things:

- You are willing to do what it takes to keep him safe even if he doesn't understand. He desperately wants to be boss, but he needs you to be the one in charge so that he has the freedom to explore and learn.
- You are willing not only to limit his inappropriate behavior but to restore him to a secure position with you. He must know (by your actions) that you love him no matter what. Remember that his cognitive abilities will only allow him to understand the most concrete expressions of your acceptance and love.
- He can have the freedom to express his feelings no matter what they are without worrying about how bad Mom or Dad will feel. Also, he can deal with his emotions honestly and appropriately without having to pay for it later by having to deal with an irritable parent.

It's all too easy to communicate our emotional issues to our children. If a particular behavior your child acts out gets to you, it's imperative that you ask why. If we don't understand the impact of our own upbringing on our attitudes, then we're likely to pass this along to our children. People who have been controlled by their parents tend to become controllers themselves. People who have been abused as children tend to exhibit abusive behavior as adults to those around them. These patterns are not inevitable, but without proactive responses they are much more likely to occur unabated.

Separation anxiety and stranger anxiety, mentioned earlier in this chapter, are connected to your child's understanding that he is separate from you and you are separate from him. These different kinds of anxiety occur after the seventh month, extending beyond the twelfth month. They are quite normal in light of your child's cognitive development.

There is probably nothing better than experience to help this fear. With each time we leave and return, our children will learn a little more about our dependability in returning to them. However, we need to express to them acceptance and firm assurance that we will return. Here are a few things to keep in mind as you manage your child's anxiety:

- Don't try to sneak away if you are leaving him in a nursery or with a baby-sitter. Give yourself enough time to deliver him and stay there while he acclimates to his surroundings. Sneaking away will only exacerbate his fear, creating a "now you see him, now you don't" situation.
- Don't pry him away from you as you are trying to leave. Attempt to create a distraction or task he can do that allows him to see you leave while assuring him you will return.
- As his language skills develop, communicate that you will be gone for a "little while," always remembering that the concept of time is probably only loosely understood.
- Even if he understands that you will return, don't expect him to like it. It's OK for him to cry. As time goes on, he will cry less as he gains a better understanding that you will return.

Stranger anxiety depends on children's increasing understanding of the familiar people in their life and their outright preference for them over others. Like separation anxiety, experience is ultimately the best teacher, but there are several things we can do to facilitate our little ones' acclimation to a stranger in their immediate environment.

Children have amazing ways to protect themselves from strangers. When our daughter Corrie began to show signs of stranger anxiety, she was clear in her disdain for strangers as she balled her little fist into a lethal battering ram, and would push up at the stranger as if to say, "STAY AWAY!" In addition, the scowl on her face would have melted steel. It was a very effective technique to get her message across. It was our job not to shame her attempts to control her world but to understand what she was going through and allow her the space to work it out.

We can help our children see that not all strangers are bad by:

- Allowing children to look over our shoulder safely at the stranger and get accustomed to his or her presence. Don't try to cajole, or worse yet, reason them out of their defensive position. Let them do it in their own time. It's OK. It's part of growing up.

- Allow your little one the opportunity to remain distant from someone you will see again. He will have another opportunity; he doesn't have to go to the person right now.
- Remind yourself that this is a normal part of his development and relax. Don't bother apologizing for his anxiety—it can too easily communicate that something is wrong with him.
- If you have the opportunity and the time, sit with someone your little one doesn't know and allow your child to get to know the person at his own pace. It will be good experience and a valuable lesson in relating to another person.

A FINAL NOTE

As I have spent the years talking to parents about raising their children, I have seen that they often get overwhelmed by the multitude of things involved in raising their kids in a healthy way. As we talk further, it becomes clear they are focusing their sights on raising more than "healthy" kids; they are trying to raise "perfect" kids.

As anyone you might ask will tell you, that's impossible. But the question is, do the actions and expectations of many parents suggest that? For the vast majority of us, I think not. We really do want to raise kids who are healthy both socially and emotionally. But in our fervor to produce this, we raise kids who are just as neurotic as us!

It's vitally important to seek to be the kind of parent who is not ashamed to deal courageously with his or her own faults. We must be willing to deal with life from a realistic perspective, and more than anything else be willing to grow with our children in their process of maturation.

It is not our job to produce the character of our children. We train them; God produces their character. This process will extend far beyond the short space of years we have with them. Therefore, let's enjoy the time we have with our children and be a "good enough" parent rather than a perfect one.

Your Child from Two Years to Six Years

Our task as parents in facilitating our children's potential gets more complicated and challenging as they reach preschool age. The more independent and volitional our children become, the more challenged we are at training and directing them toward using their developing skills. The key to helping our children reach their potential is learning the balance between doing things for them and letting them discover how to do things for themselves.

Our children may help us by their demands to do a task by themselves. These demands are your first cue to back off and let them experiment with their own skills and abilities. Some children may not be quite so vocal about doing the task themselves. These kids need to be encouraged to try while their parents slowly withdraw their input. For whatever reason, these children are not convinced they can manage alone. In this case, the job of the parents is to stand by and cheer while offering the necessary encouragement to keep trying.

One way to see our job of facilitating our children's potential is to think of a teeter-totter. Imagine that the left side of the teeter-totter represents the percentage of responsibility you have throughout the life of your children. The right side of the teeter-totter is the increasing age of your child. The teeter-totter itself represents the shifting weight of responsibility from you to your child. For a good part of your child's first six years of life, your end of the teeter-totter will carry most of the weight. In other words, you carry most of the responsibility for your child. Your responsibilities do not change much during this time, yet you still need to be looking for ways to make your child increasingly responsible for himself.

As with any teeter-totter, the balance is never complete. There are constant adjustments. At times, our children may handle the shifting weight quite well. At other times, they may blow it and not handle it so well. Sometimes we'll have to move the teeter-totter back toward more responsibility for us and less for our children. This is not a time to yell and shame our kids or get disappointed in how poorly they are doing. It's a time to remind ourselves that growth and taking responsibility has its ups and downs, and our children's behavior is showing us they can't handle certain responsibilities just yet.

On the other hand, when they handle their responsibilities effectively, we need to continue to shift the teeter-totter in their direction. Our goal is to keep ahead of our children—shifting the responsibility to them just ahead of what they can handle, but not so far that they get discouraged. At the same time, we have to give them enough responsibility to motivate them to become "big" like Mom and Dad.

How does this analogy fit preschoolers? Preschoolers are constantly on the move, jumping up and down on their end of the teeter-totter, constantly demanding more responsibility for themselves. One of my daughters, Anne, was three years old when she decided it was time that she zip up her coat. When this happened, I had a choice to either ease up on my end of the teeter-totter and let her have that responsibility or push down on my end of the teeter-totter and demand that I do it because she didn't know how.

The issue was that she needed to try. She needed to be convinced that she needed help. At the time, I had enough foresight to give her the opportunity to prove herself. She tried and couldn't manage it. Her little, stubby fingers just couldn't operate the stubborn zipper. She cried briefly and then offered the zipper for my assistance. It was an important lesson for both of us. I needed to give her the right to try to be independent, and she needed to test her abilities. It wasn't a setback that she couldn't operate the zipper; it was a mile marker telling her that she just wasn't ready yet.

Don't get me wrong. She didn't stop trying to zip her own zipper, and eventually she was able to do it. It was an equally important mile marker for me to let loose of the reins a little and let her deal with her own limitations and learn how to ask for help.

The challenge during this next period of growth in our children's lives is to learn how to let them explore and grow while staying close enough to facilitate the learning process in the best possible way. Kids function best with fences. They need to have their areas of exploration marked out for them, and then they need to be let loose to learn all they can.

Chapter Seven

Feelings?...
What Feelings?

Intellect is to emotion as our clothes are to our bod-
ies: we could not very well have civilized life without
clothes, but we would be in a poor way if we had only
clothes without bodies.

Alfred North Whitehead, *Dialogues of Alfred North Whitehead,*
as recorded by Lucien Price

Many people I talk to see emotions as dispensable. They feel it's the intellect that counts.
Emotions are simply gushy, sentimental, and useless. They're
something God could have left out of our dispositions. I'm convinced these same people feel this way because of how threatening
their own emotions are to them. They make such generalizations
so they won't have to be surrounded by people who have the
emotions they would rather not feel themselves.

When these same individuals become parents, they find themselves in a predicament as they confront the emotions of their
two-year-old. Here is one author's description:

When people ask the age of my younger son, Jake, I have only
to answer "two-and-a-half" to receive a sympathetic, knowing
smile. "Oh, yes," they nod. Even those who know nothing else
about children have heard of the "terrible twos."

But to me the twos are not as terrible as they are terribly
enigmatic, a time of alternately thrilling and exasperating

extremes. However well a two-year-old may walk or even talk—however much he resembles a miniature adult—he is a walking transition: no longer a baby, not quite a child.

Just up from her nap, my daughter sits on my lap and softly cries, "I want my mommy." She tries to push her way into my very body, to crawl back inside. She is seeking some abstract mother, some enfolding presence from which she can never be taken. I kiss her gently. "Don't kiss me, Mom," she says, indignantly wriggling out of my arms, trying to wipe the kiss off her cheek.[1]

What an apt description of the dilemma in which a parent finds herself as she tries to cope with her child's roller coaster emotions. It does no good to say that emotions are dispensable right now. They are there whether we like it or not, and our job is to try to teach our kids how to cope with them in healthy, appropriate ways. At the same time, our teaching must be geared to the level at which our children are functioning.

During the preschool years, our children pass through two phases of Erikson's stages of psychosocial development. Erikson explained a child's emotional development in terms of the crises he must resolve as he grows. For the first two- to two-and-one-half years your child has dealt with trust versus mistrust, and autonomy versus shame and doubt.

The next stage of emotional development spans the ages two to six years. This stage is called *initiative versus guilt*. This stage is an outcome of children's expanding cognitive skills and physical maturation. As they grow physically stronger, they become able to accomplish more. That's one reason that children during this stage of development are so action oriented. They enjoy the fact that they can do things with no one's help (autonomy). Not only that, they become more aware that people have different motivations and perceptions than their own.

Erikson remarks that "initiative adds to autonomy the quality of undertaking, planning, and 'attacking' a task for the sake of being active and on the move, where before self-will, more often than not, inspired acts of defiance or, at any rate, protested independence."[2] In other words, prior to this stage, your little one was more likely to defy your instructions out of a desire to have his own way. Now, as he progresses through this stage, his protests to your instructions and limits may come more from a plan of his own, rather than simply an assertion of wanting to do something opposite of what you want.

Understandably, there is a down side to this kind of initiative—an increasing understanding that the actions they would like to do are wrong or disobedient. This invokes a sense of guilt. As they carry out actions of their own planning and initiative, they find there are some consequences they don't appreciate. As children learn to manage these conflicting feelings, they learn to balance initiative with self-control. This process occurs within the context of a safe environment, which their parents provide, for experimenting with these extremes. As they experiment, an explosion of negative feelings arise.

I HATE YOU!

One of the most distressing of these emotions or negative feelings is aggression. It can come in a variety of forms, but no matter what we see, we are alarmed at the intensity of these emotions within our children. Where did this come from? You might say to yourself, "I didn't teach him that!"

Aggression arises out of children's newfound understanding of the world around them and their renewed efforts to control it. As they begin to understand they can accomplish certain things to their satisfaction, invariably they bump into their limitations in spite of their confidence that they can get the job done.

One day a friend of mine was sitting in his living room reading when he heard a blood-curdling scream from his two-year-old boy's room. His mind immediately leapt to a variety of catastrophic thoughts—someone had crept in the window and was trying to kidnap his son... or he had fallen off the bunk bed. He imagined a dozen other scenarios. As he walked into the room, he relaxed as he saw his son beating a toy on the floor. He was distressed, though, at what he witnessed. Where did his son learn such unrelenting aggression? My friend had worked overtime not to model such behavior to his son.

"What's wrong, Joe?" he asked.

The little boy through his tears and frustration said, "Top won't come."

"Here, let me help you," my friend responded as he took the toy. He quickly undid the top to his son's absolute amazement and joy.

His son's world was in order again. Daddy had saved the day. This is an example of what psychologists call *instrumental aggression*. It is, at times, an explosion of frustration and anger at an object. This kind of aggression includes the conflicts you witness between children—arguing over who goes down the slide first, grabbing toys from each other, pushing another child out of the way to get on a swing. This aggression is object oriented.

Generally, we don't need to worry about this kind of aggression. It is simply a child's frustration when a plan is thwarted or he is physically unable to carry a plan to a satisfactory end. If it looks like your little one is on his way to overcoming the obstacle, even through his frustration, let him finish the job. If he's getting so upset that he's losing his ability to accomplish what he's after, then it's time to intervene as my friend did.

Another type of aggression is called *hostile aggression*. This kind of aggression is person oriented. It is directed at other people. This is classic bully behavior. It's the kid who does hurtful things to other kids just to be mean and express his anger.

This kind of aggression can come out in verbal ways as well. If you've ever stood on the edge of a school playground, you'll know what I mean when I say that at times kids are the most cruel creatures on earth. There is no limit to the verbal abuse they heap on each other. They haven't learned the more subtle ways to hurt others that adults have learned to use, so they do so with incredible ruthlessness.

Hostile aggression is often expressed by screaming and verbal attacks. It goes beyond cutting comments (although this is included) and is an all-out attack on another person's character. It often doesn't have to be provoked by the person who becomes the object. It flows out of the feelings brewing inside the person expressing the aggression.

Usually you will see your child's aggression as a response to your limit setting. This has typically been called simple *defiance*. He may have a temper tantrum, go to his room and slam the door, or respond with a sarcastic comment. As children grow, this kind of aggression seems to move from instrumental aggression (getting angry because he can't do something) to hostile aggression (attacking others). The key to helping your child express emotions in a healthy way is to teach him how to control his anger and vent his emotions without resorting to hostile aggression.

The one thing we do not tolerate with our kids is what we call "cutting someone down," or character assassination. This is verbal aggression that attacks who a person is, rather than attacking what the person does. This kind of attack usually results in a quick swat or time-out, depending on the degree of "assassination."

One morning an explosion erupted between my two oldest girls, Corrie and Anne. It quickly deteriorated into a shouting match about their ugliness, and other unseemly comments about each other. I could have matched them with my own shouting and anger, but this time I didn't. I separated the combatants and let them sit while I cooled down. Then I decided on the consequences.

All too often parents react to their children's verbal aggression with their own anger. This results in more hurt feelings rather than a constructive conclusion in which everyone learns a little more about respecting one another.

If we act impulsively in response to our children's aggression, we're teaching them how to meet aggression and suppress it. On the other hand, if we first stop the aggression, and then consider the consequences for our children, we slow the sequence of events and are in a good position to teach them about respecting others.

I'M AFRAID, DADDY!

The ages two to five years are by far the most fearful for your child. This fear has a lot to do with a change in a child's thinking at this age. They are moving from the immediate and concrete to the imagined and abstract. As their new cognitive powers take hold, they can hold pictures of things in their minds. They can take events they have seen and experienced and create new and frightening variations. Kids can also create their own scenarios that are just as frightening as the things they see in the real world.

The frustrating part of a child's fear and anxiety, as one parent said, is "I just can't talk sense to him. I show him there's nothing to be afraid of, but it just doesn't seem to help!" Our frustration results from a lack of understanding of the preoperational thought of two- to six-year-olds. Logic and reason will not allay their fears. Their thought processes are not yet developed enough. Many conclusions children make about the world are based on their random observations. They base their conclusions on a sequence of events in time rather than understanding true cause and effect.

I'm sure you've seen parents try to get their child to overcome a fear with exposure to that fear. If you've ever been to a petting zoo, you've probably seen a parent holding a wailing child as they approach a goat or some other animal. To an adult's mind, it only makes sense that if you expose yourself to your fear and see that it isn't dangerous, your fear will go away. Unfortunately, this process doesn't work for two- to six-year-olds.

Little learning takes place in the face of abject terror. Keep in mind as you work with your child's fears to follow and lead simultaneously. The parent at the zoo could have stood at the gate of the animal pen with her young boy and talked about the goat while letting him see others pet the goat. Occasionally, she might have asked him, "Do you want to go see the goat?" If he had said, "No, I don't want to Mommy," that's OK. The next time they went to the zoo, she could go a little farther into the animal pen, stand closer to the animal, and do the same thing (this is the leading part). In time his curiosity would get the best of him and he would be ready to approach the animals.

What is crucial here is allowing our kids to master their own fears rather than pushing them beyond fear simply because they should know better.

MASTERING THEIR EMOTIONS

The key to enhancing and further facilitating your child's emotional health lies in your ability to balance freedom and responsibility. For example, if you say that hitting someone is inappropriate, you've set up an outside boundary for your child. You must also say, "When you get angry, you should walk away and give yourself time to cool down." Often parents fail to instruct children in the appropriate behavior, yet they hold them responsible for it. The thing to be careful not to do is to add further restrictions to your child's emotional displays. Your child will learn how to balance self-control with emotional expression within the confines of his freedom. If everything is disallowed, how can he learn?

The teeter-totter metaphor, discussed in the introduction to this section, provides a key to helping our kids develop emotional health. The older children grow, the more our role becomes that of a "consultant" helping them manage their emotions. As they continue to learn self-control, the responsibility for their emotions should progressively shift to them. What this means is that if your child explodes at a limit you have set, and you know that he has learned some simple ways to deal with his frustration over your limits (walking away, going to her room), then you should expect him to use these ways to handle his anger.

Let's say your son asks to go out to play, but it's too close to dinner time and you say no. If he storms to his room and stays there to cry, yell, and just lick his wounds, that's OK. That is an appropriate way to handle his emotions (particularly for a five-year-old). It tells you he has learned that exploding in your face really doesn't accomplish anything, and he may say something he will regret. Therefore, he withdraws to regroup emotionally.

I have seen too many parents prohibit emotional displays, thereby communicating that emotions are not tolerated. The next time your boss says no to a request for a vacation you were really counting on, watch what you do. If we expect our kids to act better than we do in response to frustration and anger, we're in trouble. It's one thing to expect more of ourselves, since we may have developed the strategies and have the emotional resources necessary to cope with such setbacks. It's quite another to expect the same from your three- to five-year-old.

Too many parents fail to recognize their child's attempt to express emotions appropriately by putting further restrictions on them. For example, when a parent says to a son as he heads for his room, "Don't you walk away from me! I'm not finished yet. You can't go to your room; you need to stay here and work this out with your sister!" the child doesn't have the opportunity to get his emotions back in order so he *can* work it out. There is nothing wrong with cooling down before we attempt to resolve a conflict. All too often we try to deal with conflict when we're the most emotionally volatile. This only leads to more frustration and failure.

I'm not saying we shouldn't hold our children accountable for the hurtful things they say or other destructive acts they display. When the situation has quieted down, it would be appropriate to sit with them and review what has happened and what could have been done differently. Remember that even in emotional times, your role continues to be the teacher-trainer, not the reactor.

If your child is only two years old, your expectations need to be different. Your expectations have to be consistent with your child's ability to handle emotions. Two-year-olds simply can't handle emotions proficiently and shouldn't be expected to. Most two-year-olds will be overwhelmed with their feelings and react impulsively and often quite vocally. That's why temper tantrums are the hallmark of this age. Here are the two most important elements in facilitating your child's emotional health:

- Accept your child's ability to handle emotions (that doesn't mean that you condone inappropriate behavior). Does your child get quickly overwhelmed by emotions and then they dissipate? If so, remind yourself that "this, too, shall pass" and give your child the space to let feelings subside while making sure he's in a safe place. Many of us have "timers" in our heads that go off and we conclude that it's time to be over whatever the upset is. Be careful. Your child probably doesn't have such a timer and will need to regroup emotionally.

  Also be mindful that once their little nervous systems get "cranked up" with emotions, they may need some help getting quieted down. This is the time to take your child in your arms. Also tell him what he needs to do to be obedient.

- Look for opportunities to teach responsible behavior in handling emotions (like being able to sit down during a temper tantrum and quiet himself, or not yelling as loudly during a tantrum, or even keeping a tantrum from lasting as long as it usually does). Be quick to comment and praise increasing abilities to overcome and master feelings appropriately.

Your toddler or preschooler will learn at least as much from your actions as from what you say. I was reminded of this one day when our daughter Corrie came upstairs to get me to fix a video tape that was malfunctioning. Her timing couldn't have been worse. I was in the middle of a writing project and didn't want to be disturbed. Reluctantly, I went downstairs with her to check it out. As I examined the hopelessly "eaten" tape, I realized this was going to take longer than I expected. I lost my cool and forcefully placed (more like slammed) the cannibalized tape on top of the TV. I left the room briefly to get some tools to extract from the VCR what remained of the tape.

When I returned, I winced at the scene unfolding before me. What I hadn't noticed was that Anne (three years old at the time) was sitting on the couch soaking up all of her dad's angry behavior. I walked in on her grabbing the videotape and slamming it repeatedly on the hearth. She was simply doing what she had seen her dad do—a sort of practice for the next opportunity when she was angry. It was a poignant reminder of the power of modeling.

Kids are into doing things. That's why actions have more significance to them. What they see done, they can do as well. The reason I go into detail over all this is to sound the call for consistency. If you are going to give your children an emotionally healthy environment and attempt to teach healthy and godly ways to handle their feelings, then you had better be ready to examine your own emotional reactions. The behavior and attitudes you expect from them need to be applied to your own life and attitudes. If you are not ready to do that, then you will teach something entirely different. You will teach them how to "talk the talk" but not "walk the walk!"

Most of us hope our children grow to be emotionally healthy people who are comfortable with themselves and confident in who they can become. Not only that, but we hope they have a sense of worth based on who God is, rather than on what people say.

Children's self-esteem and sense of worth are built in the "small" experiences with their families. That doesn't mean that the big events of appreciation for who they are and their importance aren't valuable. But when you look back over the years for the significant experiences you had with your parents, you might be surprised to find that the big events don't jump to mind. It's the times spent in the car together or doing some seemingly insignificant shared activity that we remember.

Just as political candidates have their "spin doctors" and "image makers," we must remember that we are our children's image makers. How we talk to them and to others about them shapes their image of themselves.

Here are some tips to keep in mind as you commit yourself to building up your children:[3]

- Recognize and support their originality and enthusiasm. Play along when they initiate a game or explore an object or idea. Encourage them when they create their own way of doing something; be patient and let them discover whether or not it works.

- Take turns with your children in talking, playing, and showing affection. The easy back-and-forth exchange you develop with each other lets them know they are important to you and you like being with them.

- Allow your children to rely on you as a resource; help them to learn the skills and information to overcome fears at their own pace. Your willingness to let them lean on you will give them the confidence to take the next step in development.

- Remind them of their capabilities—the words they understand and the strengths they have shown in the past in coping with their feelings, solving a problem, or being creative.

- Provide opportunities for self-expression: read books, draw, or paint pictures together; have frequent conversations and be sure to ask questions. Let their interactions—with people and objects—teach them.

- Show true admiration for who they are. Let your children know how happy you are that they are part of your family. Use words and actions to communicate "I like being with you, I like who you are, and I want to spend time with you."

- Acknowledge, respect, and respond to your children's right to have their own thoughts and emotions. Help them express difficult feelings, but never take away permission to have them.

- On occasion, become a follower so they can experience being a leader. For example, if you go for a walk in the park, let them choose which path to take.

- Set limits that are clear and predictable; offer to help them as often as possible to succeed in doing what you want them to do. When you must lay down the law, do it in ways that ensure they understand that you are rejecting their behavior but not rejecting them. When you have particularly difficult times, take the initiative to make up so they will know you still love them.

• When you pray with them, talk to God about them mentioning specific, concrete things you are thankful for and things they have accomplished.

Thankfully, our kids' emotional development doesn't depend solely on us. It's consoling to remember that God is working with us to train our kids. If that reality weren't supporting my efforts, I think I'd give up.

Encouraging our kids to be emotionally healthy people is a challenge. We need to teach them that feelings are OK but not to vent on others. We have to balance this by teaching them to use their developing cognitive abilities to negotiate and get along with others. And we need to participate with them in their learning how to master their emotions while not getting our emotions tangled up with theirs.

Chapter Eight

Look Who's Talking!

M̲ost of us can probably remember the movie *Look Who's Talking*. It's an amusing story of a toddler and his thoughts (all verbalized) about people and the world. The humor of this film is in how well it captures the looks, sounds, and stares of kids in response to the world around them. Kids don't have the inhibitions of adults in their evaluation of people and situations. They unabashedly comment about how stupid something looks or they laugh at things. Most adults have too much decorum to respond so freely.

From ages two to five a child's vocabulary explodes. Tom and Nancy Biracree point out in their book *The Parents' Book of Facts* that "the average child understands about 300 words and uses about 50 at age two. That vocabulary soars to 1000 words at age three, and 8000 to 12,000 words by age five. A typical five-year-old's vocabulary includes most of the words he'll use for the rest of his life."[1]

YOUR CHILD'S LANGUAGE DEVELOPMENT

Language fulfills many needs for our kids, among them these four:

The need to describe their world. Once children pass the milestone of their first words, they must continue to find a way to gain the words necessary to label things. Even after developing their first meaningful words, they still have a long way to go to be able to communicate what they see to the people around them.

The need to relate to others. Children have to develop not only the repertoire of words necessary to describe their world but the understanding of how to use words effectively. This is the "me" and "we" of language in which they express themselves—what they feel, think, and experience. It can also be used to enter into a relationship with another person in a meaningful way. They can use words to express love, displeasure, and concern for another person.

The need to find out why. Children need to develop the language skills necessary to find out about their world by asking questions. They will find out that they can benefit from the experience of others rather than always needing to experience for themselves. As annoying as it is to parents, they will develop the unique skill of asking "Why?" With this simple question, they not only find out how their world operates, they find the words to describe that world and influence it in a meaningful way.

The need to regulate. This need extends not only to things but to people—both themselves and others. They will find out that words not only describe their world, they also control things. Words can control another's actions when they convey a need for something and get that person to do it for them. This is learned very early when parents become miraculous mind-readers able to understand their children's grunts for everything from a pacifier to a teddy bear. Still, children need to develop action words to get people to do things for them in more specific ways. After all, grunts don't accomplish very much after the parents begin to wise up!

Children will also learn to regulate and control their own actions by their ability to talk to themselves. They will find that words direct their own actions as they talk themselves through various activities. As I've stood and watched my daughters play, I'm fascinated by how they talk to themselves. One day I overheard Corrie say to herself, "Now don't do that, because if you do, it will fall and you'll have to do it all over." It sounded surprisingly like something I would have said to her.

That's the way children learn to regulate their behavior—they learn to talk themselves through it by modeling the instructions they have learned from us. Later, this lays the foundation for a whole array of "self-talk" that becomes a more sophisticated means of controlling adult behavior.

LET'S TALK

How do we keep up with our children's exploding language skills? Here are several ideas.

The fine art of conversation. There is nothing more valuable in helping your child develop language skills than conversation. Nothing fancy, just plain conversation about anything and everything. It may be a little difficult to carry on a meaningful conversation with a two-year-old. But over time, if we lay the groundwork for talking about things, it will be even easier when they are five and six years old.

For two-year-olds, talking means expanding their telegraphic speech and labeling things. Telegraphed speech occurs when they condense a longer sentence into a few words. These sentences get progressively longer as their command of words continues to develop.

Our youngest daughter, Abby, is quite enamored with our golden retriever whom she has affectionately named Shisha (her real name is Sunshine). We jokingly describe Sunshine as the only dog who has an eating disorder. Sunshine will eat absolutely anything. What this means is that Abby has a golden shadow who follows her when she walks around with food in hand.

One day, Abby came running into the kitchen screaming "Shi-sha nanni!" It was like the world had fallen apart. What had happened was that her shadow had nabbed the banana she was carrying and had lain down momentarily. In reply, her mother said, "Did Sunny eat your banana?" When Linda did this, she expanded Abby's description of the situation and filled in the language gaps.

Recently, Abby was again toddling around with the ever-familiar banana in hand and decided to give it to Sunny since she didn't want to eat it. She looked for our approval. Upon receiving it, she held out her hand trustingly with the banana in it. Not one to look a gift horse in the mouth, Sunny took her cue and gobbled down the banana. Immediately, Abby beamed and retorted, "Shisha eat nanni!" It was a momentous event in our house, since it marked the movement from two-word telegraphed sentences to three-word sentences (still telegraphed, of course).

That is probably the extent of how parents help their toddlers expand their language skills. We need to label things for them and get them to label things by asking, "What is that?" If they come up to get their daily vitamins and point to a purple vitamin, we can say, "You want the purple one?" The more we practice this, the easier it comes. With each exposure to more words, they pick them up and begin to use them.

As children grow older, we can ask them to describe experiences they have had. For example, talk to them about the last visit to the park or zoo. Encourage them to tell who wasn't there. We may have to say, "Tell Daddy about the geese we saw in the park." As they launch into their story, we will probably have to help them to unroll it. For example, "What did the geese do when we got close?"

As children approach preschool age, we can begin to engage in more active forms of conversation, posing more open-ended questions. It's still important to help them label what happened to them. They may give us the facts of what happened—one of their playmates ran home. With specific questions, we will give them further elaborative abilities by asking, "Was Tommy angry when he ran home?" As a follow-up, we may want to ask them how they felt when Tommy ran home.

Answering questions. When little ones begin to ask questions, they are beginning to realize there's a world out there that might be interesting and worth finding out about. It marks a move from their egocentric world to a wider one full of experiences and objects to explore.

The way we go about answering questions will also be a large part of their language development. Remember that all conversation is a learning experience for your child, and even as we answer their simple why questions we increase their ability to describe their world and relate to us at the same time.

Besides these two important aspects of language development, there is also the element of teaching them how the world operates and what to expect from it. This heightens their ability to control it and feel better about themselves.

Have you ever wondered how your kids developed the amazing capacity to ask questions that stump you? There are probably two reasons for this. First, as parents we are stumped by the task of explaining something complex to a three-year-old. Therefore, when we reach for the words to translate, we get stuck. Second, unknowingly your child may be asking something that is unanswerable, either because they are tapping the edges of human knowledge or because they are tapping the edges of your knowledge.

A few things to remember:

- When children ask "What's that?" they are probably asking us to help them remember the name of an object. They are probably not looking for an explanation of the inner workings of it. For example, your child may ask "What's that?" pointing at the microwave oven. The simplest answer is to name it for them and leave it at that. If they continue, there is something else they want—like more time with us. If so, then we may need to redirect them toward another activity or object.

- Try not to fall back on "Because that's just how it is." If the question is answerable, answer it briefly in concrete terms of what it does.

- Don't bother mustering up everything you know about the workings of a microwave and how it cooks food. Children are very egocentric, and the only thing that matters to them is how an object relates to them, not necessarily why it does what it does.

- Be sure you know what kind of information your child is looking for and what she can handle from an intellectual perspective. One young mom told me the story of her three-year-old daughter who asked her, "Where did I come from?" This mom took a deep breath and began to tell an abbreviated version of her daughter's birth and other related details. As she was doing so, her daughter's faced changed from interest to exasperation.

  "No, no, Mom. Where did I come from—Chicago or Denver? Sara says she came from Denver. Where did I come from?"

Teaching relationships. Another way to expand children's language skills is to show them the relationship of things to other things. For example, you may be looking at a photo album with your child and say, "Grandma and Grandpa are your mom's daddy and mommy."

Teaching how things or people relate to one another will help children grasp other relationships such as opposites, things that are similar, and things that are related because of their qualities. In terms of how we measure intelligence, these concepts are vitally important in learning to reason with language. We must never forget that everything we do is mediated through language. Therefore, the more exercise we give our kids to use language to understand the world, the better prepared they are for future endeavors of reasoning and other logical skills.

Reading interactively. Reading activities are so rich it is hard to estimate their value. Reading should become part of your daily routine with your child. The one request from my girls I will rarely refuse is to look at a book. As they get older, this becomes more of an undertaking because my job shifts from just naming items on the page to encouraging them to "read" it for themselves. Eventually, this leads to them reading to me.

For the younger child, read interactively. This will take the form of pointing to objects on the page and asking what they are. It will also include naming objects. A great example is an animal sounds book. You can associate sounds with the objects in the book. Early on, your little one may be better at giving the sounds of the animal than the name, but as their language skills progress, they can bring these together to say what it is as well as the sound it makes.

As children get older, we can begin to read to them and they can enter the world of words that actually describe things they know. As you pick out books to read to your child, remember that they will be most interested in things they are familiar with. Therefore, be sure to get books that have items in them they may have seen, touched, or tasted.

Children who are four and five can probably begin asking questions about what you've just read. Their abilities to remember things will have increased by this time, and as you review, you are further building their vocabulary words for labeling things.

Creating words and stories. Encourage your child to write stories or draw stories for you. The older our daughters became, the more interested they were in communicating their thoughts by writing or drawing. Corrie is very good at drawing a picture and then telling a story about it. This kind of exercise encourages not only imagination but the selection of words to relay their inner worlds. As they grope to come up with the "right" word to explain their picture, we can jump in and help them add another useful word to their vocabulary.

As your children get older, involve them in writing notes to people or writing something to Mom or Dad for their Christmas card.

Reviewing experiences and events. Engage your child in debriefing. What this means is that you review the event in which they've participated. One of our daughters, Anne, is in a tumbling class. The rule for the class is that parents have to wait outside until class is finished. This gives us an opportunity when she comes out to ask what happened, and it gives her the chance to explain all the new things she's learned.

Reviewing experiences and events will exercise and facilitate a child's memory for events, give him an understanding of sequences, and develop more words to describe what he has done.

Everything we do with our children contributes to their language development. This perspective keeps my wife and me from being overwhelmed. If you remember just one thing from this chapter, remember to keep talking to your children. They need your narration of the world. This is a vital link in building their language skills.

Words and language are the vehicles by which we can bless or "curse" each other. Your child will be watching how you handle your words with them and with others. If you talk to them and others respectfully, they are likely to do so themselves. If you talk to others one way (nicely) and to them another way—they will do the same. They will find out all too soon the powerful effect words can have on another person. Give them the gift of using their language skills to build others up rather than tear them apart.

"Reckless words pierce like a sword, but the tongue of the wise brings healing" (Prv 12:18).

"A man of knowledge uses words with restraint, and a man of understanding is even-tempered" (Prv 17:27).

Chapter Nine

These Shoes Are Made for Walking (and Running)!

A s children move out of the toddler stage and into the preschooler stage of development, their motor skills gather considerable speed, both figuratively and literally. For most of the first year, they are relatively stationary, and our ability to exercise their gross and fine motor development is within easy reach.

From the moment they take their first steps, their gross motor development picks up speed. Kids not only cover more territory, they need more supervision and involvement from their parents to direct this energy toward constructive potential.

From our children's birth to two years of age, our ability as parents to entertain and facilitate their motor development has been quite manageable within the confines of our home. When children hit the period from eighteen to twenty months and beyond, they need more space and variety to develop their budding motor abilities. This requires more planning and careful scrutiny of their toys to encourage the vast potential that resides within them.

Children also need the kind of activities that facilitate their fine motor and adaptive skill development. In chapter 5 we divided up motor development into three categories: gross motor development, fine motor development, and adaptive skill development. Fine motor development and adaptive behavior are even more important during these years because of kids' increased abilities to ambulate and discover new things. Their potential to discover their world greatly expands compared to their experiences from birth to two years of age.

Fine motor development and cognitive development go hand in hand. In order for children to develop the mental images necessary to interact effectively with their world, they have to develop the means to get information into their system. The use of their hands and fingers is vital to shaping their thinking about the world. Their hands and fingers give them new and exciting information about the materials they handle and the things they touch, taste, and smell—both good and bad.

As a toddler grows up, many parents change their focus from the child's motor development to mental and intellectual development. This shift away from motor development may be one cause for one of the least physically fit generations of elementary school children in America's history.

One set of authors puts it this way:

Only 2 percent of 18 million young people passed the Presidential Physical Fitness test the last time it was administered. A study of 18,000 young people by the Amateur Athletic Union found that only 36 percent met the fitness standards for "average healthy youngsters." Forty percent of those surveyed had at least one risk factor for cardiovascular disease. Poor physical fitness is largely a result of lack of exercise, which in turn comes from a long-term failure to encourage gross motor activity.[1]

Although the trend is heading back in the direction of physical fitness for preschoolers, there are at least three reasons why we shift our focus away from gross motor and fine motor development. Many parents don't understand the relationship between gross and fine motor development and intellectual development. They don't understand that a child's development is interconnected, and when one system is encouraged and facilitated, all bodily systems benefit.

Children's movement in space and the use of their limbs gives their brains the stimulation to continue to form mental images to understand their world. That doesn't necessarily mean that if you focus on this area and exclude the others, all the other areas will benefit. It simply means that their hands, limbs, and other body parts are important conduits through which information about their world flows. Remember, toddlers and preschoolers are most interested in doing things, not just hearing, tasting, and seeing them. They learn about their environment when they act upon it.

The second reason for the shift away from encouraging motor development and physical exercise is that it requires time, supervision, and planning.

As my girls have grown, one of our favorite activities is to go for a bike ride. When they were smaller, it wasn't so bad—I just packed the two into the little kid trailer and took off.

Now it's more of an ordeal. First I have to get my eldest daughter's bike out and make sure the tires aren't flat. Then we have to put helmets on, get the necessary books to carry along in the Burley (the kid trailer), and bring a diaper bag, water bottles, baby wipes (in case of a natural disaster), and bandages (in case of any spills along the way). That takes about an hour! Then we get on the trail, and begin our long awaited bike trip. Twenty minutes into it, someone is picking on someone else in the trailer. Thirty minutes into our trip, my eldest daughter is getting tired of peddling. Fifty minutes later we return home to give the glowing report of our outing! We spent almost as much time getting ready as we did actually riding.

A third reason for the shift from encouraging physical skills and motor development is related to something I've been bringing up throughout this book—boundaries. How does this relate to encouraging your child's motor skills? Most often it relates to parents who are too fearful of their child getting hurt.

Part of our heritage as parents no matter what kind of family we have come from is a desire to give our kids something we never had. Often, this something gets translated into overprotectiveness—an unwillingness to allow your child to risk new behavior, particularly behavior that is physical in nature. Because a parent doesn't want to see his child hurt, he refuses him the opportunity to learn and exercise new physical skills. Sadly, the issue here isn't the child's welfare (although that is certainly part of it) but the parent's pain at seeing their child hurt.

One mom I talked to chalked up her unwillingness to let her son get involved in sports to competition, which in her mind only led to injuries. To her, injuries were bad and should be avoided at all costs. Because of her unwillingness to allow her son to try such activities, he lost the opportunity to explore further the use of his body and the excitement that comes with controlling one's body to accomplish things. She simply couldn't see how not letting him experiment with his physical abilities was related to her fear for his safety and her unwillingness to deal with her own feelings of fear if anything were to happen to him while she was supervising his play.

In the end, she wouldn't loosen the reins, and the little boy had a constant shadow following him wherever he went. The really unfortunate thing is the message it communicated to the little boy—you simply can't take care of yourself and must have me to protect you from yourself.

Motor development will contribute to physical fitness in later years, and it facilitates your child's intellectual development. Without the experiences that come from the use of motor abilities, your child will be robbed of valuable information about his body and the world around him.

LET'S BOOGIE!

When I was a teenager, we had a phrase that usually meant the beginning of fun— "Let's boogie!" That phrase may date me, but it's an apt description of how your toddler feels—"Let's go; it's time to run and play!"

As your child grows, he will need more "acreage." If you have a big yard, that may be relatively easy to achieve. If you don't, be sure to find the nearest park. Children need space to practice their running, walking, jumping, and other gross motor skills that really don't require anything more than space. As they move farther away from you to play in a sandbox or just explore among the trees on the edge of the park, they are teaching themselves about their environment and creating important mental images of their world.

Your child will also need more equipment than before. From

about age three and beyond, such equipment includes climbing platforms or swing sets with various attachments, ride-on toys, push/pull toys, and things to catch and throw. You may want to start saving for a swing set. Most children love the sensation of swinging with their parents, and eventually will want to do it themselves as they grow more independent.

If you can't get this equipment, don't despair. Most cities have parks with playgrounds that do have this equipment. Or go to a local school playground with your child. Some cities have playgrounds subdivided with a special area set aside for toddlers— lower platforms, lower swings with special harnesses that fit around your child's waist, and lots of sand to play in.

Your focus will be on gross and fine motor activities. Monkey bars and swing sets are the kind of equipment you can encourage your little ones to experience that will enhance their gross motor development. For fine motor development, use a sandbox with lots of toys that require the use of your child's hands and fingers.

Finally, children need supervision from their parents. Just how much supervision they need will of course depend on the situation and the kind of child you have.

Once, when my wife and I sat watching our kids play, Linda pointed out a couple who were attempting to supervise the play of their two children. As we watched, the mother followed her daughter no matter where she went. If she went to the play equipment, the mom was there hovering. If her daughter headed to the swings, she was a ready playmate to swing her. They didn't exchange a word. It was as if the mother were a silent sentry of her child's physical safety.

The effect of this "hovering" behavior on the child was interesting. Compared to many other kids on the playground, including our own, this child seemed much more reckless and needy. It seemed with every play equipment change there was something she "needed" from her mother to help her play there. The child was less concerned with her own safety because she knew her mother was always close by to "save" her.

Where is the balance between this mother and a neglectful one? Let's go back to my teeter-totter metaphor. The starting place always depends on what your child can handle. As you watch your child play on the playground, slowly back away. Generally speaking, children are quite cautious about their physical safety. Be on the lookout to decrease your level of involvement in his independent play. He needs to learn how to be responsible for his own safety, and he can't do that if he knows you will do it for him, like the mother in our example. At the same time, you need to be ready to intervene when you think he is getting in over his head (climbing too high, not seeing the hazard he's stepping on). Even so, your voice may be more effective than your nearness.

Children this age need space, equipment, and varying degrees of supervision. Keep these in mind as we move to some specific things you can do. Below is a list that includes the kinds of toys you may want to consider. These will be divided into gross motor and fine motor development aspects of your child's overall motor development. Helpful for developing gross motor skills are:

- Climbing equipment and swing sets. These items can get quite expensive. Compared with other playthings, though, they will pay for themselves many times over in terms of use. This kind of equipment will give your child practice at climbing and developing balance, and will give large muscles the necessary demands to grow and become stronger. Swinging teaches physical coordination in the use of legs and body (learning to "pump" to keep swinging without adult help). Swinging also gives valuable stimulation regarding a child's body in space. As I've commented before, gross motor activity is useful to develop not only physical skills but also intellectual development in creating mental images of high and low and movement.

- Wading pools. A wading pool provides stimulation—the feeling of water on the skin, the feeling of movement in the water that builds strength, and an understanding of the location of the child's limbs in space.

  Include playthings in the pool to stimulate fine motor development. Floating boats and other toys will help in this development. Many suggestions for water toys given in the first section of this book apply during this age as well.

- Trips to the park. Children need variety just like we do. Even if your child has a swing set, an occasional trip to the park provides a break from routine. Parks have different swings, more sand to play in, and more kinds of climbing activities than your child is used to.

- Balls, bats, balloons, and other throwing and catching toys and equipment. These items provide upper body exercise and further learning in hand-eye coordination.
- Big Wheels and other riding toys. These provide large muscle development in the legs and trunk.
- Games. In "Follow the Leader" have your child imitate your actions. Some ideas to try: swing your arms, kick your feet, jump with both feet, stretch your arms over your head, stand on tiptoe, wiggle your fingers, lean to the right and to the left. Then let your child have a turn being the leader.

  In "Jump the River," place two pieces of string side by side on the floor to form the banks of a river. The space between the strings is the water. Show your child how to jump over the water without getting his feet wet. You can make it into an imaginary land and a great pretend game in which both of you can play. Be sure to tell him to watch out for the alligators! As his strength improves and he gets better at jumping, you can begin to move the banks farther apart.
- Modeling healthy modes of physical exercise. As noted in previous chapters, our children are watching us and how we conduct our lives. Modeling plays a big role in your child's love for activity. Exposing my kids to bicycling even before they could ride laid the groundwork for their love of riding their own bikes.

Promoting children's fine motor development requires a wider range of materials and activities than those needed for promoting gross motor development. Children's museums and well-run preschools are great sources of assistance.

Children's museums provide a place for exploration through various exhibits and activities.

When we lived in Indiana, we often went to the Children's Museum of Indianapolis. At that time we didn't have children, but we went on the annual field trip with the school in which my wife taught. The kids looked forward all year to this event because they got to do things they would never get to do at home or school. This museum had areas to explore the properties of water, a place to demonstrate the qualities of electricity, and one exhibit (one of my favorites) that had a computer that answered questions for "his" devoted crowd about the various workings of a computer.

Large metropolitan areas usually have a children's museum. If you are not near a large city, it might be helpful to call your park district or YMCA to get a lead on an activity center for children.

A well-run preschool is also a valuable experience for your child as he approaches school age. A well-stocked nursery school has a wide array of material and playthings for your child to use. The staff understands the need for fine motor development and will engage your child in such activities as cutting with scissors, painting, pasting, working with clay and Play-Doh. A good preschool should have play equipment and materials that are different from those at home. The teachers should be experienced at planning games, songs, and other activities designed to bring pleasure to young children. Check with friends who have older children to see what they did and if they sent their kids to a preschool. A personal recommendation remains the best assurance of quality of a good preschool program.

You can do the same type of activities at home with:

- A painting set of water-soluble paints
- Play-Doh to make various shapes and forms
- Sewing cards. They can be purchased at any toy store or school supply store. They usually have a storybook character on the front, and the shape of the character lined by holes in which your child can "sew" a piece of yarn.
- A small sand box. This may be an item you have to save for, but it will provide hours of fun and interest for your child.
- Blocks, "bristle" blocks, Duplos, and Legos. All these would classify as building materials to create different shapes and objects. They encourage imagination and use of the smaller muscles in the hands and forearms. Legos are more appropriate for older children because of the smaller size of the pieces. Even older kids, though, enjoy Duplos and can make some very imaginative designs with them.

As your children grow beyond toddlerhood, their motor development continues to be an important area of focus. Although the more exciting changes have passed, they will need to be encouraged to do things that facilitate their continuing development. The refinements they make during the next few years before they finally go to school will be vital for their adaptation to a changing world and crucial to their intellectual development.

My wife's family had several traditions centered on activities together. For example, their Thanksgiving tradition was to get up and have a great big breakfast and then get their hiking boots on and go out to the beaches of Lake Michigan. She has fond memories of going out to see the lake "kicked up" and watching the breakers come in. It was great fun and good exercise on a day when little exercise usually occurs.

To capitalize on our children's natural desire to move and exercise their bodies, we need to get out to be a part of that experience with them. What kind of lifestyle legacy do you want to leave behind—couch potatohood or a fun lifestyle that encourages activity?

Chapter Ten

Reality— What a Concept!

Comedian Robin Williams once proclaimed, "Reality—what a concept!" in one of his famous running monologues on the nature of people and how they deal with their world. He spoofed the fact that some people act as if reality were something they could toy with rather than live.

For children from ages two to six years, reality is a concept. They think they can shape reality at their whim. Their reasoning abilities simply aren't developed enough to realize that some things are constant.

It's important to remember that from ages two to five, children go through a period of intellectual transition. The conclusions they reach about reality and other aspects of their world are often faulty and sometimes humorous, like this one:

One morning an elementary school teacher asked her class how many points a compass has. She was surprised when one little boy stuck up his hand and said, "Five." She asked him, "Five? What are they?" He counted them off: "North, south, east, west, and where I am."[1]

Remember the research of Jean Piaget with his children and others? He looked at childhood intellectual development in terms of stages. Toddlers are in the preoperational stage. During this stage they develop the ability to think of the world in mental images. What this means is that they can describe some event or object without having it in front of them. This milestone shows they can now store and recall these mental images. This process of storing and recalling is called symbolic thought. In other words, preschoolers can use symbols (the mental images) to represent what is in the world around them. It marks the beginning of their reasoning abilities that will continue to be refined over the next several years of life.

Our daughters showed this development of symbolic thought when they could look at our golden retriever and say that she was a dog. The next time they went to visit their grandparents and saw Grandpa's border terrier (a much smaller dog), they could say that she, too, was a dog. There is more to this thought process than meets the eye. A child has to have an image of "dog" in mind to compare with what he sees. When he makes this comparison—four legs, tail, ears, elongated nose, sniffs a lot, jumps up on you—he can make the accurate conclusion that this, too, is a dog.

There are four aspects of this stage of intellectual development: self-centered perspective, focusing on one aspect of an object, inability to change the form of objects, and concreteness.

Self-centered perspective. One Sunday as I was driving home from church with Anne, our four-year-old, I asked her if she was in the same class with another little girl whose parents I had met that day.

She looked at me quizzically, and said, "No, I'm not. But she's in my room!"

Small children can't see the world in any way other than from their own frame of reference. It's not because they are selfish; it's simply a part of their maturation to see the world in this way. Another example of this is the young child who believes that his fourteen-year-old babysitter is a "big person." Later, if you refer to the babysitter as a "kid," you may get a strange look because he fully expects you to see the sitter as big too.

Another aspect of this self-centered perspective is that your child attributes his feelings and motivations to inanimate objects.

For example, his teddy bear will get hungry and the sun will disappear because it is going to sleep. He will attribute his feelings to others as well. If he is hungry, then others are hungry.

Focusing on one aspect of objects. Children tend to center in on one aspect of an object and ignore all other aspects of that object. Let's say that you show a child a tall, slender glass filled with water and then take that glass and pour the contents into a short, wide glass. After you finish, you ask the child which glass held more water. The child will tell you that the tall, slender glass held more because it is "bigger."

Inability to change the form of objects. If our four-year-old is served a pancake cut into ten pieces, she's convinced she has more pancake than she did when her mom first plopped it on her plate. In other words, she can't transform the single pancake into many pieces and see it as the same pancake. This inability to transform objects holds true although she watches me cut the pancake into the pieces.

Concreteness. You can't use abstract concepts to explain a situation or object to a toddler or preschooler. If you referred to someone you had met as "cold," your preschooler would be convinced that person needed to stand in front of a heater to get warmer. They are bound by what they can take in with their senses.

As you can probably imagine, if you thought the way preschoolers do, you would make some critical errors in thinking. One significant error occurs in how they understand cause and effect. Children form conclusions based on random observations. Often they rely on the fact that two events happen in sequence to form the conclusion of cause and effect. One example might be the young boy who thinks something bad about his mother and the next day something bad happens to her. In his reasoning he is likely to think that he caused that bad thing to happen to his mom.

Children from divorced homes often believe that because they heard their parents fighting over their discipline they are responsible for their parents' divorce. To their way of thinking, if they are the object of the argument, they must be the cause of the problem between their parents. Wise are the parents who can help their kids understand reality, even if it is from the limited point of view of a preschooler.

HELPING THEM THINK

Although much of your child's intellectual development is genetically determined, you can still capitalize on the abilities God has given him. For example, one characteristic consistently found in households that produce gifted children is an enriched environment where the parents encourage creativity, self-expression, exploration, and independence. The kids in these kinds of homes have certain God-given abilities, but their parents are quite active in encouraging their development.

Variety and challenge are also found in these homes. Your child will get bored with any task he masters. Therefore, you need to find some way to keep the things he does just ahead of what he can actually do. Challenge has to be balanced against his abilities so that the challenge doesn't get so great that he becomes discouraged and gives up.

Finally, opportunities are the staple of intellectual development. What this means is exposure to a variety of places where learning can take place, such as museums, zoos, preschools, Sunday school, walks with your children, and trips to the playground.

I had a friend in graduate school whose father wrote to him on a regular basis. One day as I strolled into his office, I noticed he had one of his dad's letters on his desk. He wasn't reading the letter, he was poring over a dictionary. I asked him what he was doing. He explained that he and his father had a little tradition between them. When his father wrote him notes and letters, he would include words and phrases he knew his son didn't know. Sure enough, when my friend received the letters, he always found a word he didn't know. He would have to drag out his dictionary to figure out what his father was saying. It was an interesting tradition his father had developed to encourage his son's intellectual abilities.

What kind of intellectual game can you develop with your child? Making learning fun and exciting is important to a child's success. Remember, at this stage in your child's life, everything is grist to analyze, explore, and understand.

Over the last twenty years, the most reliable predictors of success in preschool and school are the parents' educational level and income level. Now, don't despair when you read that statement. Success in school doesn't have to be connected to educational level and income. These aspects were identified because of the kind of values such people typically hold: encouragement to try new activities, stretching their children's horizons by exposing them to new experiences, communicating the need for education for further advancement and opportunity. Of course, income allows parents to afford their children more opportunities than most, but opportunities don't have to be elaborate for children to learn.

My father and mother were both high school graduates, and for most of my growing up years their income level was modest. Yet my parents valued reading and education. They provided me with the foundation and motivation to pursue levels of education far beyond theirs. I include this example to show that income level and educational level are not necessary conditions for your child's success in school. What is important are the values you communicate about education and the opportunities you make available to your child that will facilitate intellectual development in the years to come.

CORE VALUES PARENTS HOLD

Significant influences of cognitive development in children are the values parents hold about school, achievement, and educational development. I was strongly influenced by the value my parents placed on education and they contributed significantly to my educational achievement.

Values reflect in everything parents do, from talking to their children, reading to them, and the activities they choose. If your focus is on learning, exploration, and creativity, then you will look for opportunities to allow these things to happen, including such things as finger painting, painting with brushes, and playing with Play-Doh.

Another thing you can do to communicate these values of exploration, discovery, and creativity is to do them with your children. When you take them to the children's museum, take part in the various participatory exhibits. No matter what you do, be on the lookout for new things.

One day as one of my daughters and I were walking our golden retriever, I heard the chirping of a cardinal in the woods. We quietly stopped, and listened and talked about the bird and what he probably looked like. Later, sitting on our deck, another cardinal came to our bird feeder. I quickly called my daughter to my lap (that way I could keep her from fidgeting and scaring the bird off) and pointed out the bird. It was an opportunity that allowed her to match the sound she had heard in the woods with the bird we saw at the bird feeder.

Such opportunities convey our values to our kids about learning and exploring the world. Your love for learning is easily caught through opportunities such as these. It's also an important way to communicate that learning doesn't have to happen only at school. In other words, our world is our classroom.

THE IMPORTANCE OF EDUCATIONAL PLAY

Never underestimate the importance of play for preschoolers. Direct interaction with their world through play produces valuable information. It allows them to create mental images necessary to perform simple mental reasoning activities highlighted earlier in this chapter. Without this information, your child may continue to make reasoning errors since they have nothing to refute them! (This doesn't mean your child won't correct these reasoning errors with age. At the same time, the more exposure he gets to deal with cause and effect, the more likely he is to develop the skill to see these things more accurately.)

Here are some types of play materials that facilitate cognitive development:

- **Arts and crafts materials.** These include chalk, crayons and markers, activities that include pasting and gluing things together, Play-Doh, finger painting, painting with brushes, and using scissors (safety).
- **Toys for pretend.** *Play.* These include Play-Mobile figures, Duplos and Legos, doll houses, dolls, trucks, cars, and various other props for imaginary activities. Don't forget clothes for playing dress-up.
- **Puzzles.** These can progress from pre-cut slots for individual pieces to real jigsaw puzzles (fifty pieces or fewer).

- **Lotto and "Concentration"-type games.** These games call upon memory and matching skills. Lotto games require a child to match a smaller card with a picture on a game board as in Bingo. Simple concentration games involve the laying out of pairs of cards with the same pictures on them. As each player turns up a card, he attempts to remember the location of cards that match. The game progresses as the cards are paired up and taken off.

- **Board games.** There are simple board games where moves are decided by turning up a card and matching the color on the card with the place the player must move his game piece. These games are helpful in learning about taking turns, matching colors, counting, and following rules.

SKILLS TO ENCOURAGE DURING PRESCHOOL YEARS

During the years leading up to your child's entrance into preschool and eventually kindergarten, you should encourage and capitalize on the following skills:

- **Colors and shapes.** As your child begins to master the use of language, you can begin to name shapes and colors for him. As time passes, ask him what shape things are and what color they are. This sets the stage for beginning classification skills.

- **Numbers.** We can thank *Sesame Street* for its contribution to teaching children to recognize numbers, colors, shapes, and letters. Each are aspects of language. Critical concepts in terms of number skills include counting orally to ten, matching numbers of objects, and understanding the concepts of empty and full, more and less.

- **Understanding opposites.** This important classification skill requires not only observational skills but following simple directions. This includes the concepts of up and down, in and out, front and back, and over and under.

- **Size.** This includes understanding what is big and little, long and short. By the end of this period, most children should be able to match shapes and objects based on their size.

- **An understanding of self.** This knowledge includes age and birthday, full name, gender, parents' names, home address, and telephone number. Besides the fact that there is survival value in knowing these things, they are important developmental milestones for your child to understand that he is a separate, unique individual apart from you.

- **Verbal, listening, and memory skills.** These include following directions, repeating a sequence of sounds (rapping on a table to see if he can imitate it), remembering objects from a picture he has seen, identifying parts of his body, and repeating a sequence of six to eight words.

This is not an exhaustive list of skills and concepts that must be learned prior to entering school, but they typify the kind of skills to encourage in your child.

A WORD TO FATHERS

There's accumulating evidence on the importance of the father's role in a child's cognitive and emotional development. Studies show a correlation between a father's nurturing behavior and his child's intellectual achievement. For example, one study examined the relationship between paternal behavior in childrearing and intellectual functioning in preschool girls and boys of varying socioeconomic classes. The researchers found there was a substantial relationship between paternal nurturance and two different measures of verbal intelligence. Among girls, it was the social class of the father that appeared to predict their intellectual competence.[2]

A father's nurturing behavior and presence have an impact on a child's mental development. Another study on the effect of father absence on the cognitive performance of six- to eleven-year-old children found that there was a depression in scores on measures of intelligence and academic achievement in white children. Black children also showed depression in their scores, but this depression showed up only in scores of academic achievement rather than intelligence.[3]

These studies suggest a correlation between father absence or nurturance and child intellectual development. This does not imply that one causes the other. It simply suggests that there is a relationship between the two. Nothing more than that can really be said, but it does give us reason to believe a father's role in a child's life cannot be underestimated for emotional and intellectual well-being.

When it comes to the area of enhancing and encouraging our children's potential, it seems that men in general function under a number of myths that hinder their attempts to assist in the area of intellectual development. Here are a few:

- "I'm not their mother. I don't have the time to do this stuff! Anyway, their mother's role is so much more important than mine." When we take our jobs seriously, we add to our burden as men. In fact, we double our burden! We not only have to work during the day; when we get home we need to orient ourselves to the job of encouraging our kids as well. There is no way to compare the role of the mother and father. But as research suggests, a father's nurturance affects kids as much as any focused effort to work on their intellectual development. It could be that the emotional security a father offers makes it possible for his children to excel intellectually.

"I'm not a teacher. I don't know how to help my kids intellectually!" You don't have to be a teacher. This myth is one I have struggled with as well, since I live with a teacher. My wife has been quick to remind me that it isn't what I do to teach my kids that will enhance their intellect, it is who I am and the time I spend with them. How much effort does it take to play a board game with your little one? It could go a long way toward encouraging his intellectual development.

"I don't know all the information about development like my wife does." You don't have to know all there is to know about development to help your kids grow and learn. Look for teachable opportunities. It may take some time to think in these terms, but once you do your child's horizons instantly expand because Daddy has become a part of them! The simple act of taking your child with you to work when you are not planning on staying exposes them to a new environment they have never known before. They get to see where you work and they will begin to ask questions. The moment they do, you have your first practice at becoming part of their intellectual development.

- "I'm not a reader. I don't like to do academic things. As a matter of fact, I hated school. How am I supposed to encourage my kids in something that I don't care for?" If you're the type of person who has never really taken to academic things, encouraging your child's intellectual development certainly presents a daunting task. On the other hand, there are things you do like to do, right? Involve your kids in those activities. They will not only have your presence, they will be exposed to new materials and activities they will rarely get to experience.

Are you beginning to get the picture? All too often we bog down with preconceived notions about structured, organized times in which our kids are supposed to learn. When we do that we miss precious opportunities with our kids. Just remember—*any* involvement, no matter how halting, no matter how flawed, will help your little ones develop. They will always be able to see past your foibles to your heart. That's what will give them the security they need to learn and grow.

> *"Teach a child what to think and you make him a slave to your knowledge. Teach a child how to think and you make all knowledge his slave."*
> —author unknown

Chapter Eleven

Me, You, and Us

Parents form their children's social world for the first eighteen months of life. No one else really matters to them. They need to understand that their parents are reliable and the world is a relatively safe place in which to live.

We've learned that children's sense of security and safety in the world provides them with the basis from which to venture out into the world of relationships with others. In order to do that they need to understand their "base of operations" is reliable, consistent, and always there for them. They need to know they can always return to this base to get their love "batteries" recharged and launch out again for another adventure.

No doubt, by this time, your little ones can tell by looking at you how you feel, and have the rudimentary skills to express their concern. They are also beginning to understand they are separate people and their feelings are separate as well. That also means they can mark out their territory and property by their favorite phrase, "MINE!"

As social awareness builds, they begin to incorporate others into their image of the world. There is a slowly developing sense of "us." There is me, you, and now us. Prior to this, they could recognize that we were separate people with separate feelings and thoughts, but we still stood as unconnected individuals in their understanding. As this stage progresses, they can understand that a relationship exists between them and others, and these relationships connect them. People are no longer objects to be used to get needs met. They are significant because they give nurturance and comfort, fun and games, and personal security.

A critical building block for social development is intellectual ability. Children have to store and retrieve the mental images of others' behavior in order to imitate them. As they do this, they can then store these images, retrieve them, and reproduce the behavior. At this point children begin to interact socially.

As their cognitive abilities process these images, they produce different behavior with which people interact. The people around them give the necessary feedback to adjust behavior the next time. In the same situation, children may "correct" their behavior to relate more effectively. As they follow this process, their social behavior shapes and molds into ways of relating to people that are characteristic of them.

As we noted in the first chapter, the social atmosphere our children enter has been shaped by us. Some of the forces that shape the atmosphere are the "unwritten rules" that we have learned exist in any relationship. These unwritten rules come to the surface most poignantly in our families.

One way to think of these unwritten rules is in terms of a "social contract." This model of learning how to be social incorporates the elements of the predominant views of socialization held today by professionals. Dr. David Elkind, child psychologist and author of *The Hurried Child,* describes it this way:

> This model argues that socialization always presupposes implicit, usually unverbalized, and unconscious reciprocal expectations on the part of children and their parents. The nature of expectations varies with the age of the children and the sensitivity of parents.[1]

The social contracts between parents and children are often experienced in terms of the expectations each have of the other. Therefore, the fulfillment of these contracts is found in the rewards and punishments used by parents to shape their child's social behavior. When these rewards and punishments work, it is because they support and represent the contract made between the parent and child. This is most vividly seen when this implicit contract is violated.

Take the example of young Bobby. His parents were working with him on cleaning up his room before leaving for school. As they focused on this, they forged a "contract." In essence they said, "If you clean up your room and make your bed, we will notice and give you lots of positive attention." One day, Bobby dutifully went about his business of getting ready for his day (he was going over to a friend's house to play), making sure his room was clean. He came downstairs and quietly ate his breakfast.

His mother noticed something different about his behavior because he was usually a chatterbox if he was going to someone's house to play. She asked what was wrong, and he sputtered back at her, "I cleaned my room and you didn't even notice!" The contract had been violated, and his behavior had gone unrecognized. Fortunately, it was easily rectified by his mother, who had the insight to take him by the hand and go up to his room.

After they arrived, she took time to talk about what a good job he had done and how considerate it was that he had done it without being asked. Being duly recognized, Bobby went on his way feeling that his concerns had been noticed and his security reestablished.

This story exemplifies what occurs socially between parents and their children. It is the vehicle through which our children learn to live with others and manage their social relationships. Bobby had only been told what was expected of him—nothing more. He assumed that some reward would come once he did what was asked. This assumption of reward was part of the reciprocal contract between him and his parents. When it wasn't carried out, he was upset about the change in the rules.

I would encourage you to go back to chapter 1 to review the kind of family you came from. It's important that you understand what you bring into your relationship with your child. It will help you choose your behavior as you train your child how to relate to others. There may be some "rules" you simply take for granted that need to be evaluated in terms of their healthiness for your family and your relationship with your child.

Rules or contracts exist between children, too. Initially, you will notice that even your toddler enjoys a playmate's company (remember he is probably still at the stage where the playmate is seen as an object rather than a person). After two years of age (approximately), true socialization occurs. From age two to adolescence, our children progressively move away from us. They spend more time with their peers and less time with us. From age two to six, play dominates the socialization with peers.

Children pass through a series of stages on their way toward establishing true relationships with each other. The first stage of play children engage in is called *parallel play*. This type of play is characterized by two children sitting together playing separately. They may be engaged in similar play activities, but little or no interaction occurs between them.

The next stage of play behavior appears around age three. This is called *associative play*. During this stage, children are more interactive with each other, and are truly playing together. If, for example, they are engaged in similar play activities and sitting together, they may talk to each other about what they are doing, and may even exchange toys. They are still separate in terms of the activity they are engaged in and the goal they are attempting to achieve.

True interactive play doesn't usually occur until after their fifth birthday. This *cooperative play* is characterized by mutually agreed upon rules, goals, and behavior. They may work together to decide who takes what role as they pretend to be on a ship in a storm, shopkeepers on a street, or saving people from a burning building.

This past summer we built a swing set that included a platform from which the kids could get on the slide. One day our seven-year-old was playing with her same-age friend from next door and our four-year-old daughter. Their developmental stages were apparent in how they played out the situation they were imagining. The two older kids were acting as if they were on a ship in a storm. They were screaming and yelling to each other as they tried to "save" their dolls from the raging sea in the grass.

Anne, our four-year-old, didn't have a clue about this game. At one moment, she would be up on the platform with them playing her own little game of swinging down to the ground. The next moment she would be running to another swing and proudly proclaiming that she was another "ship" trying to help the older girls. Of course, as siblings often do, her older sister would have nothing to do with such an idea. As far as she was concerned, Anne could have floated to Borneo!

As you can see, play is an important part of learning how to relate to others. There are rewards and punishments in children's interactions that help to shape more appropriate behavior and extinguish those forms of behavior that are alienating and isolating. Much of play's value lies in providing kids with a safe atmosphere in which to experiment with new forms of behavior and adjusting them without severe consequences.

LEARNING TO BE SOCIAL

There are several things we can do to help our children learn how to relate to others in a healthy way. As children grow, our role will become increasingly one of consultant, coach, cheerleader, and safety net.

If, for example, you see your little girl beginning to engage in associative play, you can expect her to interact minimally with her nearest playmate and, if her playmate is lucky, occasionally exchange a toy with her. Don't get upset if you see the other child wistfully looking over at what your child is playing with. Your impulse may be to take it upon yourself to make your little one "share" the toy. Resist the impulse and let them work it out. They aren't at the cooperative play stage, and it is unrealistic to expect them to play that way. Sharing is still foreign at this stage.

Keep in mind their intellectual abilities, since social and mental development are so intertwined. If your child is still in the egocentric stage of cognitive development, it makes sense that he will have a tough time understanding the world from another person's point of view—like how his playmate felt when he hit him. That shouldn't prevent you from talking about how to behave toward others (in very concrete terms—"It's not nice to hit people") and what might happen if he chooses to treat people that way ("Terry won't want to play with you anymore").

More than anything else children need lots of practice and exposure to other kids. The suggestions in the chapter on social development are still relevant for your toddler or preschooler. Children won't learn to relate very well without practice. But remember that part of socialization practice includes mistakes and heartache.

BALANCING YOUR LEVEL OF INVOLVEMENT

Remember the teeter-totter of responsibility? That metaphor is key to understanding your level of involvement in your child's social life. Ultimately, your child is going to be responsible for his own social relationships. Yet, when he is young, you are going to have to evaluate your involvement based on his abilities.

Your first response when you see or hear a conflict with a play-mate brewing is to wait. I must admit, this decision is the hardest for me because I'm often not around to see my kids' ability to resolve conflict. Therefore, my wife will rein me in so that my daughters have the opportunity to resolve their differences. If you see that the conflict is getting beyond a workable level (maybe because of your child's mental abilities, or one kid is getting too upset to participate effectively in resolution), then it's time to intervene.

On the other hand, if you see that they are continuing to nego-tiate and attempting to come to some resolution, then let it go. It may not end the way you would prefer. In view of the big picture, though, the greater number of positive resolutions children expe-rience with their peers, the more likely they will persist in future conflict situations.

Children are establishing conflict resolution patterns that will continue throughout their lives. It's important they experience enough success with conflict resolution so that they won't be daunted by the next conflict to arise.

I've seen too many parents parachute into their child's social relationships to make sure nothing "bad" happens to their child. In so doing, they effectively cut off his learning opportunity to see a conflict to a conclusion. In the end, he learns that if anything interpersonal gets too "hot" he can count on his parents to save him. That's not the kind of contract you want with your child. You want him to begin to experience relational success on his own.

Interestingly, that kind of contract teaches your child to with-draw in order to control a "bad" social situation. As he comes to count on you to bail him out, he will withdraw from the situation as he waits for you. Eventually, even though you are not there to rescue him, this behavior becomes his usual coping mechanism in interpersonal conflicts.

Do we want to help our kids in the long run or right now? If the goal is to help them in the long run, then we will allow our end of the teeter-totter to creep upward, and just see how they do. If they do well, we maintain the balance there and look for the next opportunity to let it go a little higher. If they don't manage well, that's OK. It's good information to have about our child's level of social functioning. You'll know next time when to intervene and help him through it.

On the other hand, if your commitment is to help your child right now, making social interactions always pleasant and rewarding, you will be very busy attempting to make the world out to be something it isn't. That's not to say you allow a playmate to beat up your child. It simply means that conflict is not the worst thing that can happen to your child. If you are uncomfortable with conflict, you will communicate that to your little one.

LETTING KIDS BE KIDS

The purpose of a book like this is to help parents adjust their expectations to their child's level of functioning. When it comes to social development, we must remember to allow our kids to remain children. Any new experience your child faces will evoke a variety of reactions, including anxiety, tears, fear, and maybe even depression. Expect it and make accommodations for it.

Even though your five-year-old may handle many different social situations—like meeting new people at church, going into his Sunday school class without crying, going to preschool, staying at grandparents' house for a few days—don't assume your child can handle more.

We need to allow our kids the opportunity to consolidate the gains and challenges they have mastered without immediately pushing for new experiences. Let them adjust to success in these arenas before launching into a new social experience that will tax them even more.

In spite of my insistence on the necessity of transferring responsibility from ourselves to our children, I believe we still need to protect their childhood. Expectations and demands shouldn't be placed on them that are appropriate only for older children. We may take pride in how competent and responsible our child may be, but there will be a price to pay.

At the center of this pride in our child's so-called "maturity" is its reflection on our parenting abilities. We sometimes assume that if our children are growing up before other kids do, we are doing a better job as a parent. The problem is that our children trust us in the final analysis to know what is best for them. Therefore, if we push them into doing things that an older child would be expected to do, they will try to do it with all their might because our approval and love are what matters. If they can get that by acting older, they will do it. They don't understand the price of taking on responsibilities beyond their age. Ultimately, they lose something when they are pushed to be and do things beyond their age.

The question we must ask ourselves repeatedly is: Are the responsibilities I am expecting of my child appropriate for his age? Here are a few unrealistic expectations for a child from two to five years of age (one caveat: these are predicated on the "average" kid, or what one could expect from the majority of kids this age).

- It is unrealistic to expect your four- or five-year-old to fly to see his grandparents alone (United Airlines guarantees to make it pleasant for them notwithstanding!).
- It is unrealistic to expect your two-year-old to take a bath alone.
- It is unrealistic to expect your two-year-old to "share" anything with anyone.
- It is unrealistic to expect your three-year-old to walk into his new Sunday school classroom without shedding any tears (depending on the type of child you have).
- It is unrealistic to expect your three-year-old to watch the baby for you while you run downstairs to get the laundry.

If you are confused and need a reality check, be sure to talk to another parent you trust. Sometimes, just talking about it with someone helps to clarify if our expectations and "contracts" are appropriate.

TALKING ABOUT THE RULES OF RELATING

Spend time with your child talking about his relationships. (This is true for children from age three-and-a-half years and beyond.) Listen to what he has to say about how he feels about his friends. Kids get most proficient with this somewhere around their fourth birthday.

One day I had the opportunity to talk to my four-year-old about a birthday party she had attended.

"So what did you do, Annie?"

"Oh, not much."

"What do you mean, not much? What did you do?" I persisted because I knew I had to find the phrase that would trigger her story.

"Well, first Chelsea and me went down this thing where you went bump-bump-bump on your stomach, and we went aaah-aah-aaah all the way down (while she related this she added the appropriate sounds they made as they cruised down the washerboard of rollers).

I had succeeded in getting her started, now the job was to keep her on track to catch some kind of sequence so I could really understand. "So, you guys went down a slide with rollers?" I asked, trying to see if I got the picture. "You guys must have really had fun together, huh?"

"Yeah, and then we..." and she continued on her merry way relating all their various adventures through the activities.

This illustrates what I mean by talking about relationships. The best questions to ask are the open-ended ones (Who? What? How?). Take the time to paraphrase what you hear them saying so that you can really get the picture of what's happening with their friends.

This activity will be valuable in your relationship with your child, in his language development of words to talk about relationships, and in his ability to classify and organize appropriate social behavior. These are all skills necessary for effective social interaction.

At times he will come home from a difficult situation with a friend and will need you to help him debrief. In other words, you will need to talk about what happened with that friend and what he could have done differently to make the situation better.

Maybe he still needs to ask forgiveness from his friend, or he may just need to let his friend have some space to get over being sad.

As your child gets more proficient in talking to you about his relationships, you will have more opportunities to teach healthy ways of relating to people. In the early part of this age range, you will need to teach and instruct him about what he needs to do the next time his friend hurts him or says something nasty.

THE ROLE OF MOTHERS

From ages two to six, children spend increasingly less time with their mothers. Of course, some of this has to do with their new ability to see their relationship with their mother mentally. That is, although their mother may not be present, they can still have a relationship with her since she still exists in their minds.

Time with a child's mother also decreases because he is demanding much more independence and time to explore on his own. This can be seen during outdoor play by how often the child returns to his mother and just how far away he ventures.

Our girls are a good example. Our nineteen-month-old stays fairly close at hand. Although she will venture away for a period of time, she always returns for a touch or brief interlude on someone's lap. Annie, our four-year-old, no sooner gets out of the car before she heads for the monkey bars or jungle gym with no concern for staying close. She will always check in to make sure she knows where we are, but it's a momentary thing. Finally, Corrie, our seven-year-old, is like her younger sister, Annie, but she looks for other kids with whom to play.

Moms need to let go of the close contact and physical dependency they once knew with their little ones. For some moms, it's a difficult transition. Unfortunately, they communicate this discomfort to their kids, who feel responsible for their mom's feelings. In this scenario, the child stays close when he should be off exploring his world and socializing with other kids.

One young mom came to me aware of her difficulty with this transition. Her little boy simply would not leave her side. In spite of her encouragement, he wanted to stay nearby so that Mom "wouldn't be sad." This came about because he ventured away from her at a playground one day and fell down. It was a natural mistake, but she just couldn't forgive herself for allowing him to fall like that. Later that night, as she told her husband, she cried softly all over again. Her son heard her from the other room and came in to see what was wrong. He was quick to assume he had done something wrong.

Evidently, from that point on he decided not to cause his mom any more heartache. It was only with experience and age that her son could leave her side and she could let him go without blaming herself every time he got a bruise. We talked frequently about her need to allow her son to deal with his own hurts, and how he wouldn't learn to do that if she continued to keep him close by her.

No doubt about it, it's a difficult transition. Yet it's vital to make this transition from dependency to independence. If you are having trouble with it, talk to a close friend and process your feelings rather than have your child make it his problem to "fix" your feelings. If you don't, it will set up a boundary problem between you and your child. He will inadvertently become your consoler and comforter. This places undue responsibilities on your child to take care of you. He needs to be free to develop his own social skills without worrying about the effect it may have on you.

THE ROLE OF FATHERS

The recent developments in the men's movement within Christianity are truly exciting and long overdue because of the emphasis on the man's role in his family and the need for his active participation in family life.

Both sexes benefit from their father's involvement. For a girl, her father is the first man she loves. From him she will learn the rules of relating to someone of the opposite sex. Although she isn't aware of the gender difference right away, her relationship with her father lays the foundation for relating to men in the future.

For a boy, a strong relationship with his dad is critical in developing an understanding of what it means to be a man—compassionate, strong, sensitive, active, and caring. His dad will model how to handle emotions, how to relate to women, and how to relate to God. He will learn that being a man means being involved or distant depending on how his father relates to him.

Fathers can enhance their children's socialization in several ways.

- Take them to their activities—preschool, Sunday school, out for breakfast before a rehearsal for the Christmas pageant. It will provide you with valuable opportunities to talk about friends and the things that interest them.

- Learn who their friends are. Take the time to listen and learn the names of their friends. It may seem like a small gesture, but over time it speaks volumes to your kids about the level of interest you have in their lives. You would do the same for many of your business contacts, right?

- Learn what they like and don't like. It's easy to engage in "Oh, really?" and "Uh huh" conversations with our kids without understanding what's going on with them. Practice this enough to be able to anticipate their reactions to various situations. It will give you an edge in your efforts to teach them new ways of relating.

- If your job makes this difficult, be sure to take some time during the weekend to ask questions about their lives.

- Play games with them that they enjoy. Make up your own games with them.

- Read to them.

Although this list represents only a sampling of the things we can do to be involved in the social development of our kids, the point is that loving our kids means being intimately involved in their lives and trying to see the world from their point of view.

RELATING TO AUTHORITY

As parents (particularly as fathers), we can never forget that we are the first authority our children encounter. The question is: How do we want our children to see authority figures? Do we want them to view these people as safe, looking out for their best interests and willing to listen to their concerns without getting defensive? The social relationship between children and parents begins the process of understanding what a relationship with God is like.

Sometimes, there are impossible balances to maintain—like being firm yet kind. But that's our lot as parents. We can give up before we start and our children will be the losers. On the other hand, we can keep trying to reflect their heavenly Father to them and leave the rest up to God.

Relationship provides a backdrop for all you do in terms of setting limits on your children. If you've worked at your relationship with your kids, then when it comes time to do something they don't like they will still know you love them and will be there for them. That doesn't necessarily mean they will like the limit you set, or complain any less. It does mean they can rest assured you will never abandon them.

THE "EYES" HAVE IT!

The most solid foundation from which your child can build his social skills is watching you. How you treat others provides him with powerful cues about sharing, caring, negotiating, and respecting others. These are all values your child will abstract from your behavior. Naturally, there will be times when he can't control his natural impulses to grab, hit, and otherwise be mean to other kids. Still, what he sees in you will continue to instruct him in social graces.

Your child's social development is key to building healthy relationships in the future. He needs to understand how relationships work and how to participate in them. Our children watch us for these cues and will start there for their experimentation in social interaction. We must always remember that our job as parents is to work ourselves out of a job. We must create a safe, firm foundation from which our children can launch into this world with a healthy, godly sense of themselves and the ability to adapt to all the world throws at them.

Chapter Twelve

Did I Do Something Wrong?

The least of things with a meaning is worth more in life than the greatest things without it. Carl Jung

What good will it be for a man if he gains the whole world, yet forfeits his soul? Or what can a man give in exchange for his soul? Matthew 16:26

"Must I tell my parents the truth about disobeying them when I know it will only get me into trouble? Should I invite over the kid next door just because she's lonely, when I would rather do something else with my time instead? Do I have to share all my things with my cousin just because he lent me his bike just once? Why shouldn't I steal a toy from this store?"[1] This is just a sampling of some of the moral dilemmas your children will face as they grow up. The foundation you give them now will enable your children to make moral choices later.

In many ways children's development and ultimate adjustment as human beings rests on their understanding of what really counts. Their total development will progress relatively smoothly without us. On the other hand, their ability to make decisions based on enduring, absolute principles is strongly influenced by our understanding of how to nurture their moral and spiritual development. As Christian psychiatrist Paul Meier comments, "We are made up of body, soul, and spirit, so if we feed a child well and use healthy psychological principles, but ignore his spiritual development, we will be developing only two-thirds of a person. Psychological development will enable our children to live in society and earn a living, but spiritual development will enable them to understand the meaning of life."[2]

To nurture children's spiritual and moral development, parents must understand how children view such abstract concepts. They don't have a clue about morality as a term, but they do understand about sharing, caring, feeling guilt over bad behavior, and fairness. In the spiritual realm, they only see God as a spiritual version of their earthly parents. Their spirituality will be rooted in what they can see and experience. How can we as parents make our moral and spiritual training effective for our children at such a young age? Let's take a look.

WHAT IS MORALITY?

At its very core, morality is the understanding of what is right and wrong, the distinguishing between the two and choosing of an action accordingly. As Christians, our morality is firmly based on God's Word and in our spiritual lives. Whether we know it or not, our morality is also strongly influenced by the traditions and spiritual heritage we carry with us from our family of origin and also our emotional dispositions. Therefore, we cannot separate the two and consider them independently. Our spiritual commitment motivates our moral behavior. At the same time, morality has been treated in specific ways in the research on the morality of children and its development.

William Damon, in his book *The Moral Child,* summarizes how morality has been conceptualized in these studies.

- Morality is an evaluative orientation toward actions and events that distinguishes the good from the bad and prescribes conduct consistent with the good.

- Morality implies a sense of obligation toward standards shared by a social collective.
- Morality includes a concern for the welfare of others.
- Morality includes a sense of responsibility for acting on one's concerns for others.
- Morality includes a concern for the rights of others. This concern implies a sense of justice and a commitment to the fair resolution of conflicts.
- Morality includes a commitment to honesty as a norm in interpersonal dealings.
- Morality, in its breach, provokes perturbing judgmental and emotional responses. Examples of such responses include shame, guilt, outrage, fear, and contempt.[3]

As you can see with even a cursory examination, the Bible gives us a sound foundation to teach our children about each of these aspects of moral decision making and behavior. Of course, this is the advantage of having an unchanging point of reference—the Bible—for choosing our behavior toward others.

MORAL DEVELOPMENT

As children grow, their understanding of spiritual things and moral dilemmas changes too. Not only that, the choices they make and the rationale they use for those choices evolve as well.

Lawrence Kohlberg, a Harvard psychologist, formulated a theory of moral development that is worth considering in an attempt to understand how your child's morality develops. His research, conducted over a period of fifteen years, proposes that moral development proceeds in a step-wise pattern as children grow and their understanding of moral issues evolves. He believes that morality "is not a bag of virtues" (honesty, generosity, loyalty, and the like) but an idea of justice that is primitive in young children and becomes sophisticated as a child passes through distinct stages of moral development.

Kohlberg proposes three levels of moral development: *premoral, conventional role conformity,* and *self-accepted moral principles.*[4] The *premoral* level, which we will be focusing on with preschool children involves two different steps each representing a more mature form of moral reasoning. The other levels do not come along until later in your child's development. Children at step one, typical of preschool and early school-age children, believe that wrong actions will result in damage or punishment. Morality is directly influenced by the potential consequences of one's actions, and these consequences are all that matter. Children at step one make judgments of right and wrong simply based on whether they get punished or not. Therefore, from a parent's perspective, we need to explain to them the need to behave on two different levels. First, on the level that they understand ("I don't want you to do that. If you do you will get a spanking"). Second, on the level we would like them to head toward ("It is good to obey Mommy because that is what makes Jesus happy").

Step two—judgment—shifts to the intention that motivates the act. Selfish intentions are often condoned on the basis of the situation in which they occur. Moral acts, at this level of moral reasoning, are often related to the satisfaction of one's needs. As you can see, the moral reasoning becomes more sophisticated than the previous step because of the cognitive and emotional aspects. Suddenly, the child is moving from a self-centered perspective to the beginnings of his ability to take a different perspective—that of the victim or individual he is watching. This perspective-taking is a critical developmental milestone in moral development because it forms the basis for empathy for another person.

Recently, my girls watched the movie *Free Willy*. The movie depicts a young boy's relationship with an Orca whale named Willy. As the movie unfolds, the wicked owner of the amusement park where Willy lives conceives a plan to get rid of the whale—to weaken the wall of Willy's tank so that eventually it will break open. Willy's young friend takes it into his hands to rescue Willy from his evil owner. As Corrie expressed her feelings about this movie, she justified the boy's behavior since his intention was to save the whale. His motive was to do something right even if it meant breaking the law—theft of the property of someone else. Her way of thinking through this moral issue displays this step in Kohlberg's system of moral development.

What we had to do in response to this was talk about obeying the law, and that this is what God expects of us even if we don't understand the outcome. To her it was impossible to understand because of the whale's need. At the same time, she did recognize (exhibiting the level of moral development she was heading into) the need to obey the law because that is our job as Christians.

Step three is characterized by "good boy morality."[5] The individual functioning at this level of moral reasoning is motivated to conform to avoid disapproval or dislike by others. Social needs and the consideration of other people enter much more forcefully into the picture at this point. This stage of moral development begins to appear toward the end of the fourth year and into the fifth year of life.

Keep in mind that children's moral reasoning isn't quite as structured and predictable as Kohlberg's theory suggests. Recent research has found that children can display empathy for another person at quite an early age, which wouldn't be predicted by Kohlberg's theory. A case in point is the example of Ruby Bridges, one of the first kids to break the school segregation barrier in the South.

A white schoolteacher observed Ruby Bridges, a six-year-old, as she walked past the heckling mob: "The crowd was there, shouting, as usual. A woman spat at Ruby but missed; Ruby smiled at her. A man shook his fist at her; Ruby smiled at him.... You know what she told one of the marshals? She told him she prays for those people, the ones in that mob, every night before she goes to sleep!"[6]

This telling example suggests that a child considerably younger than Kohlberg's theory predicts could have empathy and compassion for those who hated her. At the same time it must be noted that her spiritual training distinctly motivated her moral behavior.

PERSPECTIVE AND EMPATHY

The last important aspect (not connected with Kohlberg's theory) in understanding your child's moral and spiritual development is the ability to take another person's perspective. It forms the basis of a child's ability to understand what another person is feeling and then respond to that. This ability is largely influenced by your children's cognitive abilities. It requires their perceptiveness to discern another person's inner psychological state. Obviously, they need to understand that others are separate from them and can have feelings different from their own. This aspect of moral development changes with age.[7]

Your child's empathy evolves with age and can be facilitated as you watch for the changes. The first developmental milestone for empathy in children occurs somewhere between the ages of one and two. At this age, we begin to see genuine concern for another person's discomfort. Besides the ability to recognize another person's discomfort, your little one may also begin to show signs of attempting to intervene to help another feel better.

By the end of the second year, your child will display an increasingly refined ability to recognize others' needs and feelings. He will also become more aware of the fact that every person's perspective is unique and that others may have a different reaction to a situation than he. Because of his increased level of perceptiveness, he will become more effective in his attempts to care for others.

GROWING SPIRITUALLY

The key to nurturing your child's moral and spiritual development rests, to a large degree, on your understanding of many of the aspects of development addressed in this book. This means that the moral and spiritual concepts will need to be simplified so that your child can understand them.

For example, helping children understand why they need to be nice to other children will be lost if you try to explain it in terms of the abstract notion of *agape* love. If you explain the importance of being nice to others in terms of how they might feel, or even how Jesus feels when he sees us treat others poorly, your explanation would have more meaning to a child since it addresses this moral choice at the level at which he is functioning.

During the years from ages two to six, your child will relate moral concepts to concrete actions in his environment. To really oversimplify it, we could say that if he acts nicely and treats others nicely, then others will treat him nicely. Going one step further, we can define what treating others kindly is—talking with a quiet tone of voice, saying "Hi" when greeting someone, thanking someone for something when they give it to you—all are concrete examples of the kind of actions that treat others with kindness.

Your teaching about how to treat others, how to think about himself, and how to respond must be termed so that you meet him at his level of understanding.

SMALL PEOPLE, BIG LESSONS

Most researchers of children's moral development have concluded that their participation in social relationships gives them the opportunity to encounter the classic moral issues facing humans everywhere: issues of fairness, honesty, responsibility, kindness, and obedience. Therefore, you don't have to go looking for an opportunity to teach your child about morality or spiritual values. They are all around. It's up to you to see them, and use them as an opportunity to teach sound biblical principles.

This orientation of seeing all of life in spiritual and moral terms was and is consistently taught by the Jews. They understood that all of life is spiritual and moral, and therefore brimming with examples and lessons to be used. Deuteronomy 6:5-9 shows just how strongly the Jews were encouraged to handle the moral training of their children:

> Love the Lord your God with all your heart and with all your soul and with all your strength. These commandments that I give you today are to be upon your hearts. Impress them on your children. Talk about them when you sit at home and when you walk along the road, when you lie down and when you get up. Tie them as symbols on your hands and bind them on your foreheads. Write them on the doorframes of your houses and on your gates.

That is our challenge as well. We must strive to see our lives in moral and spiritual terms. This doesn't mean spiritualizing our lives to avoid harsh realities that are a natural part of living in a sin-tainted world.

One family I saw in counseling had a spiritual explanation for everything. This included each others' poor behavior, forgetting things, and difficult circumstances. The trouble with this wasn't that they saw the spiritual side of an issue—I totally agreed with their explanations most of the time. The problem was, they used this spiritualizing to avoid the nuts and bolts of their relationships together. Once their son was venting his frustration about his relationship with his father with his mom present. As he did so, she got increasingly uncomfortable. When he finally paused to take a breath, she calmly looked him in the eye and said, "Well, Josh, I guess you should go home and pray about it because I can see that Satan is telling you lies about your father."

Unfortunately for Josh, in spite of the truth in the suggestion his mom was giving him, it effectively "shut him down" from feeling or talking any more. There was no more discussion, no more to be done. It is the use of spiritual truth to avoid the difficulties in our relationships that contaminate our children's view of spirituality and truth.

On the positive side, it means communicating that everything about our lives and the decisions we make has moral and spiritual implications. You can do something as simple as talking with your four- or five-year-old about what Jesus would do in any given situation. What's effective about this approach is that it gives your child a concrete reference point in the person of Jesus to help him judge what is the good and kind thing to do.

TOTAL LIFE EXPERIENCES

You've probably realized by now that the main source of your child's moral and spiritual learning is his total life experiences. Gary Collins describes it this way: "A 'loving heavenly Father' is foolishness if the child's earthly father is harsh and unkind. Even the child's view of God, Heaven, angels, and hell are in terms of pictures he has seen."[8]

Always remember that it's impossible for you not to teach morality and spiritual values. You will do it either by default or intent. Your decisions and actions are watched and recorded as a base from which your child will make efforts to fashion his own moral actions. What facilitates this is the mix of your attempts to talk about the situations your child faces and his own sense of fairness and what is right.

This is also true of your spiritual life. Kids are always fascinated with how we live out our Christianity, and we need to be sure to show them. That doesn't mean that we pray in the middle of the living room just to show them how you do your quiet time (although that may be appropriate under certain circumstances). It means that we make no effort to hide what we are doing when we pray or study God's Word. Corrie, my oldest daughter, once interrupted my wife's quiet time. Corrie asked Linda what she was doing and my wife replied, "I'm reading my Bible."

"You arrrrrre?" my daughter asked with a note of surprise in her voice. "How come, Mom?"

"Well, it's my way to learn what God has to teach me about getting along with you and your sisters, and getting along with others. It is my way of listening to God, like when you sit and listen to your Sunday school teacher."

It was one of those big lessons from a seemingly insignificant moment in time. There was nothing insignificant about it.

TEACHING PERSPECTIVE TAKING

Remember that the ability to take on another person's perspective forms the foundation for empathizing with others. One way to teach perspective taking is to engage children in role-playing characters from fiction or real life. This is one parent's description of how she did this:

> There was certainly a change in my two youngsters' understanding and behavior when we did a little role playing at home. On two different weekday mornings they took turns playing the parent while the rest of us were "the kids." After dealing with their sibling and parents complaining, "I can't find my other shoe," "The scrambled eggs are too hard," "Where's my book report?" both Alison and Andrew in turn began to sound just like Mom and Dad, making such familiar statements as "Wait a minute, I can listen to only one of you at a time," "I can't do everything," "I only have two arms." They learned more about pitching in from those two mornings than from Mom and Dad lectures.[9]

You can also teach by looking for examples of other kids who feel a wide array of feelings, and asking your child to put himself in the other child's place. Then you can ask your child what it might feel like to be the other child. Remember that this skill probably won't develop until sometime around his third or fourth birthday, but you can instruct on this even when they are younger. Say something like, "Don't hit your sister, it hurts her when you do that."

WHAT'S YOUR STYLE?

Like it or not, our kids will see God and his relationship with them through their relationship with us. They will learn about grace, mercy, justice, love, and consequences through their interactions with us. They will then apply their understanding of these concepts (in concrete terms, of course) to their relationship with God. If you are loving, reasonable, fair, and flexible in setting firm limits while allowing your child to experience the consequences of his bad choices, he will view God that way. On the other hand, if you are demanding, inflexible, and shaming ("Why did you do that? You can be so stupid sometimes!"), that is how he will see God.

Interestingly, secular researchers consistently conclude that an *authoritative* approach to parenting is the preferred approach to enhance and nurture your child's moral growth. This is characterized by a firm but flexible approach to parenting. The authoritative parent maintains ultimate control but encourages the child to develop independence by permitting and respecting choices within an established framework of values and rules. What's interesting about this conclusion is that it coincides with a biblical approach to parenting—love with limits and consequences without exasperating our children (Eph 6:4). This authoritative approach is as biblical as anything secular can be without explicitly mentioning biblical values!

Two other parenting styles have been identified. The *authoritarian* parenting style is demanding, inflexible, and domineering. The person considered an authoritarian parent is one who is convinced that he must control his child in all aspects—thinking, behaving, and feeling. Unfortunately, it robs the child of the opportunity to learn from life's lessons, because he has a parent who will not allow any mistakes, and when he does make mistakes that same parent is harsh, blaming, and not grace-giving.

The laissez-faire style of parenting is unwilling to accept the responsibility of setting limits on the child's behavior. It is one that has been characterized as permissive and lax. There is a basic belief underlying this approach that parents are to direct and nurture a child's natural bent toward good. Yet researchers have concluded this is the worst kind of parenting style for nurturing moral growth because it is only within the limits and consequences set within a context of acceptance and love that moral reasoning, moral emotions, and behavior are enhanced. Leaving children to their own devices to learn moral lessons is like leaving an infant on a busy crosswalk hoping he will find his way across the street!

TEACHING SPIRITUAL LESSONS

Any chapter on spiritual development would be incomplete without some mention of the multitude of books and other media available to teach moral and spiritual lessons. We not only need to be on the watch for daily experiences to teach spiritual and moral lessons, we need to make time for more organized teaching and instruction on spiritual concepts and values.

One only has to walk through a Christian bookstore to see all manner of books available for kids and parents, from a child's first picture Bible to videos and everything in between.

The key to taking advantage of these materials is to be prepared to use them as a springboard rather than as the teacher. None of them can replace the interaction between you and your child. You will need to be prepared to read a story and take some time to talk about the story to see just how much your child has actually absorbed. If he hasn't absorbed anything, then you will need to simplify it as examples from his own life. The examples from the preceeding chapters about facilitating your child's language and cognitive development can be applied here as well.

Your child's moral and spiritual development is a multifaceted aspect of his overall development. It is vital to motivate behavior that is caring, empathetic, and exhibiting of Christ's love. Spiritual development forms the basis for understanding purpose in life and the deeper meaning to all of life.

Our job as parents is a big one—reflecting God to our children, living lives consistent with our teaching, and teaching values that will last a lifetime. Nothing short of God's grace and power is needed to participate in such a monumental undertaking. It's daunting, but our God is great!

"Being confident of this, that he who began a good work in you will carry it on to completion until the day of Christ Jesus" (Phil 1:6).

Chapter Thirteen

Making Sense of It All

There are no ordinary people. You have never talked to a mere mortal. Nations, cultures, arts, civilizations—these are mortal, and their life is to ours as the life of a gnat. But it is immortals who we joke with, work with, marry, snub, and exploit—immortal horrors or everlasting splendors.

C.S. Lewis, *The Weight of Glory*

A wesome isn't it? As parents we are in the business of rearing no mere mortals: we are raising the future, and what a burden it can be! When I'm arguing with one of my daughters, I would scarcely blink at the thought that I'm dealing with an immortal soul. She is someone for whom I will be called to account for what I did to show her a view of the eternal. She is far from ordinary—something I would say about all of my daughters. Each is unique, wholesomely different, and exceptional in her own special way.

That's how we must approach nurturing our children's development. We must never violate their uniqueness and differentness for the sake of a theory or an expert's evaluation. We must be committed to searching out and developing a way of dealing with each child that respects and enhances the beautiful qualities God is building into them.

183

This book artificially divides up the personality of children. Rarely do any of the areas of development evolve separately. Instead, they are wondrously intertwined so that as we build in one area, we build in all other areas.

To divide your child's personality into artificial areas of development destroys the wonder. For example, the moment we chart a territory it seems to be much more understandable. The problem is that it gives us a false sense of knowing the charted territory. We can chart anything, including the entire globe, but can we really know it?

The same is true about children's development. Although we can describe specific aspects of it, we can't facilitate all of it. Enhancing our children's development is just far enough out of our reach that we can't do it alone. We need God's help. There can be no other way for us or our children to be emotionally healthy.

There's another danger of which you should be aware. That danger is communicating the idea that enhancing and nurturing your child's development can be like following a cookbook to produce a superkid. Can you see it? Here's a possible recipe:

- 2 emotionally healthy parents from non-dysfunctional families
- 1 part exercise and physical training
- 2 large measures of mental training for good cognitive skills
- 1 good heaping measure of social opportunities
- 3 heaping measures of spiritual training
- Work together for ten to twelve years
- Let rise and "foment" for the next five to six years, kneading periodically to keep under control.
- Take out finished product and send to college!

Sounds like a page right out of Aldous Huxley's *Brave New World*, doesn't it? The purpose of a book like this isn't to communicate that if you do all the things suggested (as if you could!) you will come out with a healthy, emotionally adjusted, physically capable kid who can hold his own intellectually.

The final danger is losing sight of the fact that we have been blessed (or cursed, depending on the day) with the opportunity to participate in the development of another person. Human development is a process we are engaged in that will continue long after we're gone. We are not here to produce a child. We are given the stewardship of a child to help, nurture, train, instruct, and direct toward healthy and godly living in as many aspects of his life as possible. We will never see the complete result of our investment and training.

The fine points of this process are not important. We can blow it on the fine points as long as we are committed to the process of training, nurturing, and guiding. That doesn't mean we can be haphazard and careless. We must be purposeful in what we do, even if we don't always get it right. As a matter of fact, often the wrong that we do is what is most useful to teach our kids. That is, if we choose to see our mistakes that way.

Remember the videotape incident with my two daughters? What I didn't tell you is that after that sequence Corrie, Annie, and I sat and talked (as much as Annie could at the time) about how to handle anger appropriately. We tore Dad's behavior apart and thought of some ways I could have done it differently. The process works if we follow it and don't try to reinvent it or do it "right." Our only purpose in participating in this process is to participate to our fullest. That is all we can do.

The most encouraging aspect of nurturing your child's potential is that he is a whole person who will benefit from all of your effort—not just part of it. God has so designed our children and the process of their development that if we work in one area, other areas will benefit as well. Isn't that wonderful?

As I sat to work on my daughter's math with her a few nights ago, I realized that more than math was happening. We were talking about math, to be sure, but we were also building a relationship. I was investing in her emotionally by the time I spent with her. I was also nurturing her language skills as we talked. I used a word she didn't understand so we talked about the word and what it meant.

In this book, we have traversed a lot of territory. Your little one has come from a helpless, dependent, vulnerable infant to a competent, mobile, independent, and self-reliant little person who makes himself known in some of the most unequivocal terms. It's been an exciting and sometimes harrowing journey. But what is the take-home message to all this stuff? How do you make sense of it all? Here are seven broad themes from this book to recap all you've read.

1. BALANCE—THE TEETER-TOTTER OF DEVELOPMENT

Balance is vitally important. Do not stray to any extreme as you nurture your children's potential. Keep challenging them in the development of new skills and abilities, but not so much that he will give up trying. On the other hand, we must be ready to re-adjust our expectations to where our children are developmentally. This means giving them time to develop further before we tip the teeter-totter a little more toward more responsibility on their part. If our children can't handle some responsibility right now, it's OK. Give it a rest for a while. Their inability to handle it is an indication that now is not the time to give them responsibility.

2. TRAINING, NOT CONTROLLING

Our role is to train, not control our kids. This means we are willing to let them experience things on their own terms and explore their world at their own pace. Parents who try to control their kids are ones who want to spare their kids from everything bad. That is not to say we shouldn't protect our children. But we have to be careful when we want to restrain or constrain our kids from doing some activity. We should always check ourselves out with someone we trust about why we're hesitant to let our kids do certain things or why we get irritated when they do certain things. It may be because of our own insecurities and fears rather than because of considering the good of our kids.

Training means giving children a clear idea of the outer parameters of our expectations for them—limits, consequences, and other directions for well-being—and then letting them run freely within those parameters. Remember, there is always risk involved in growing. If we do our job at giving them a safe arena in which to grow, we reduce that risk so they can benefit from their experiences.

3. PROCESS, NOT PRODUCTION

Always remember that, as parents, we are engaged in the process of training and nurturing kids. We are not in the production business—that is God's job. Therefore, we can't get caught up in the details and mistakes of how we are nurturing our kids. We must always keep the big picture in mind. There is no right way to raise a child. There is a way that fits your children and their unique abilities and temperament. It is your job to learn what that way is and keep using it to help them learn and grow.

A book like this gives you suggestions and appropriate reference points for helping you understand your child's development, but in the final analysis it is your relationship with your child that will teach you what really works to encourage the potential that lies hidden within your child.

4. WORKING YOURSELF OUT OF A JOB

During your children's early years of life, you don't have to worry much about your job security. Your children need you, period. As they grow and strive for more independence and autonomy, are you ready to work yourself out of a job? From watching some parents, I would conclude they plan to be with their children for the rest of their lives!

We're working ourselves out of a job if we really want to launch our children into the world with the skills necessary to survive. That means continuing to look for ways to shift the responsibility from us to our children for their well-being. That includes the physical (tying shoes, washing his face, brushing his teeth), emotional (learning to comfort himself to sleep), intellectual (working out a puzzle on his own without help), and the social (working out a conflict with a peer).

This also means conveying to our children a sense of values and morals that are biblically based—something they can count on that is separate from us. These values form a standard that never changes and an acceptance of them that never wavers. We must strive to plug our kids into God so that when they grow away from us, it will be a natural transition to move from under our wings to under his "wings." "Have mercy on me, O God, have mercy on me, for in you my soul takes refuge. I will take refuge in the shadow of your wings until the disaster has passed" (Ps 57:1).

5. ESTABLISHING APPROPRIATE BOUNDARIES WITH OUR CHILDREN

This concept is vital in nurturing our children's growth. When they can understand that they are separate from us, they will begin their movement away from us. Healthy boundaries between parent and children provide the basis upon which your children can learn about themselves without having to worry about you. That may sound calloused, but we must strive to not confuse our kids into thinking our feelings and worries about their growth are their responsibility. Children need to understand where they begin and end as individuals emotionally, socially, morally, and spiritually.

6. TURNING MISTAKES INTO OPPORTUNITIES

To be the best parent you can be, and to encourage your children's potential, you may need to develop a new view of making mistakes. It's a view that needs to be communicated to your child as well. It's a philosophy that makes mistakes an important part of enhancing your children's growth. Your mistakes and theirs are vital to making the changes necessary for more effective behavior and an understanding of the world.

If you can model the importance of seeing mistakes as something normal and to be expected, you will have accomplished much in a world where perfection is expected and even applauded. I'm not saying we should be careless in what we do as parents, but we shouldn't get too concerned with the mistakes we make.

What's important is what we communicate to our children about them. Are mistakes the worst thing that can happen to a person (as shown by how we react when they make a mistake or have an accident), or do we learn from mistakes? Do we apologize when we do something to hurt our kids? Or do we conveniently overlook it except when they hurt us, and then demand an apology?

7. KNOWLEDGE, NOT PERFECTION

One of the most valuable philosophies of life other than commitment to Christ is to be a learner. That is your job as a parent— to keep learning and striving to understand your child. You don't have to be the best parent, just one who is learning and willing to learn about your children. If you take that perspective, your children will grow and blossom into all that God wants them to be. Remember, your mistakes and your successes in nurturing your children will be used by God to make them into the people God wants them to be.

The key is relationship, and it can be applied to any age. Some of the most meaningful times I can remember are when my dad took me out to practice my football skills. We would go to a field next to our house, and I would punt the football to him. He would pass it back to me, all the while yelling instructions and encouragement.

On the surface, the psychologist in me would say that my father was building my motor skills, my intellectual abilities, and contributing to my moral development through teaching me to persevere to learn a difficult skill. All those things are true, but there was something more that can't be as easily identified. It was found in the relationship we were continuing to build.

My father was telling me I was important to him when he came home from a grueling day at the steel mill to take me out and throw the football around. No doubt he was as exhausted as I am (probably more so, considering the nature of his work) when I get home from work. That awareness had a lasting impact on me.

The best gift you can give your children is time with them encouraging, interacting, supporting, and teaching them. The relationship you build with them will form the foundation for everything else they achieve. The dividends of your investment will be far-reaching and eternal.

Appendix A

A Month-by-Month
Tour of Your Newborn[1]

MONTH ONE

Even the healthiest newborn may have an unearthly look about him: a wizened little red face, pointy head, spindly limbs that may tremble and shake, bumpy or peeling skin. Although helpless now, except for sucking and grasping reflexes, he will grow very quickly.

By the fourth week's end, he can probably:

- Focus on your face, crib toys, and mobiles.
- Calm down when you speak to him gently and hold him upright against your shoulder.
- Startle, cry, or quiet down in response to loud or sudden noises.
- Turn toward your voice.
- Make an "ah" sound when he sees your face and hears you speak.

Encourage your baby by showing him the world is a warm place. Cuddle, soothe, and respond quickly to his needs. He doesn't need a cribful of bright toys yet. Your face and voice are his most fascinating playthings.

MONTH TWO

Your baby is settling into recognizable eating and sleeping patterns. Prepare to be captivated by his first real social smiles when he is about six or seven weeks old.

By the eighth week's end, he can probably:

- Smile in response to your smile.
- Begin to track an object with his eyes.
- Make a variety of gurgles, grunts, and humming sounds to express his feelings.
- Lift his head 45 degrees when lying on his stomach.
- Recognize breast or bottle and squirm eagerly for it when he is hungry.
- Bat at a toy with his closed fist.
- Keep his head up when held in a sitting position, with occasional bobs forward.

Encourage your baby by acknowledging his new, sociable moods. Smile and talk to him frequently. When you pause, he will "answer" you by smiling and cooing. Show him musical toys and help him play with and track a rattle. Watch his signals. If he starts turning away or closing his eyes, it usually means he's had enough stimulation.

MONTH THREE

Increasingly aware of his surroundings, your baby scrutinizes toys and objects, his hands and feet. He is beginning to have more control over his limbs—much to his delight—and may spend a great deal of time kicking his legs and batting at objects. Encourage his physical freedom by letting him play on a soft rug that is protected by a clean towel or blanket.

Note: If your baby has been colicky, crying spells should begin to diminish or even cease near the end of month three.

By the end of this month, he can probably:

- Lift his head up 90 degrees when he is on his stomach.
- Bring both hands together.
- Laugh and chuckle.
- Smile at you from across the room (his distance vision is improving).
- Roll from stomach to back.
- Enjoy playing, and he may even cry when interrupted.

Encourage your baby by giving him just a few playthings at any one time so that he won't be overwhelmed. Make sure that all objects near him are clean, safe, nontoxic, and too big to fit completely into his mouth.

MONTH FOUR

Your baby is growing ever more enchanting. By the end of this month, he begins sleeping a decent stretch at night and has a predictable morning and afternoon nap time. When he is up, he is likely to be bubbling with pleasure and good spirits. He is starting to realize that he influences the world around him and will try to figure out how one action affects another. Don't be surprised to find him banging a rattle or dropping a toy over and over again just to see what happens.

By the end of this month, he can probably:

- Roll from stomach to back and back to stomach. He may even use rolling to get closer to things.
- Put everything within reaching distance into his mouth—a sign of exploration, not teething.
- Increase his sound repertoire by blowing raspberries, shrieking, chuckling.
- Hold his head steady when held in a sitting position.

- Grasp and shake a rattle.
- Reach for an object, although he often overshoots the mark.
- Be fascinated for minutes exploring his own hands.

Encourage your baby by introducing games such as "This little piggy" and pat-a-cake. Help his language skills along by imitating his sounds. He will love it and answer back. He will also enjoy such exercises as being gently pulled into a sitting position.

Note: Do not turn your back on him even for an instant while he is on a bed or changing table. At this age, he is very likely to roll off!

MONTH FIVE

Your five-month-old is reaching accurately, using his hands to explore the world, and rolling with ease. His physical activity helps strengthen his muscles in preparation for sitting and crawling, although for some babies this goal is still far away.

By the end of the month, he can probably:

- Briefly sit in a tripod formation (legs spread wide apart, leaning on arms for support).
- Lift both arms and legs in a Superman pose while he is on his stomach.
- Do modified push-ups and make swimming motions with his arms and legs.
- Delight in his own reflection.
- Enjoy rhythm and music.
- Become increasingly adept at bringing objects to his mouth for oral exploration.

Encourage your baby by continuing with gentle sit-ups. Vary sit-ups by pulling baby up into a standing position. To help him stay balanced while he sits, place a favorite toy or book in front of him. Read him a book with bright illustrations. He'll particularly enjoy simple poems or rhymes.

MONTH SIX

Big doings are ahead this month. Your baby is sitting up without help and may even have cut his first tooth. He is increasingly able to express his feelings, especially his positive ones about you. His whole body radiates joy when he sees you! He may raise his arms to be picked up, snuggle against you, and reserve his best smiles for you alone.

By the end of the month, he can probably:

- Sit independently.
- Push up on hands and knees in a crawling position and rock back and forth.
- Make consonant-vowel sounds such as "ba," "ma," "pa," and "do," and put them together in long, melodious strings of gibberish.
- Hold his own bottle.
- Show a certain amount of wariness in front of strangers, and may cry when you leave the room.
- Begin to pass objects from hand to hand.
- Support most of his own weight when held in a standing position.

Encourage your baby by playing "Peek-a-boo" to reinforce the idea that you can go away and come back. Take him out a lot, and introduce him to other children (but don't expect him to play with them). Help him strengthen his legs by occasionally holding him in a standing position when playing.

Note: Electric cords and outlets pose serious hazards. Provide a safe environment for your little explorer by baby-proofing your house, if you haven't already done so.

MONTH SEVEN

By the end of this month, your baby is really honing his skills. He is standing with support, vocalizing, and improving his hand-eye coordination. He'll probably be teething, too. Expect the bottom two front teeth to poke through at six and a half to seven months, followed by the top two teeth four to eight weeks later. If he has shown previous signs of stranger anxiety, he may be even more wary now. Your baby may also be increasingly clingy and upset when you leave the room. This type of behavior is a sign of separation anxiety and is a normal developmental stage.

By the end of the month, he can probably:

- Stand with support.
- Sit comfortably and steadily.
- Go from a sitting to a crawling position.
- Communicate some of his basic needs.

Encourage your baby by not keeping him cooped up in a playpen; he needs plenty of room to roam. Offer him soft, rubbery toys to chew on to help ease teething discomfort.

MONTH EIGHT

Your baby is increasingly independent but may also be very clingy when a stranger is around. His sleep pattern may be disturbed by his fear of being alone. He will call out to you for reassurance. In spite of his stranger anxiety, he will probably enjoy spending time with another baby.

By the end of the month, he can probably:

- Feed himself a cracker or small pieces of food.
- Look for a dropped object.
- Take sips from a cup (but expect spills).
- Crawl or creep–but not necessarily in the direction he wants to go
- Pull up into a standing position.
- Use his index finger to poke at things.

Encourage your baby by clearing breakables off low tables and keeping closets and cabinets locked to give him free movement around your home. You might consider giving him his own kitchen cabinet and filling it with plastic and lightweight metal pots, pans, and utensils. If he doesn't know how to get down from a standing position, help him bend his knees so that he can lower himself to the floor without falling. A routine (bath, story, song, and a firm but loving "night-night") will make bedtime easier. A familiar blanket or cuddly toy can also be a big source of help and comfort; safeguard this important object!

MONTH NINE

Your nine-month-old is making both physical and intellectual strides. He is playing in an entirely new way: using two toys at the same time, beginning to stack and sort objects, putting small toys in a pail or pot. He can also understand more words and gestures, so keep him busy in conversation. He may oblige your request of him to wave bye-bye or play "So big."

Note: Look for the appearance of his top and bottom lateral incisor teeth. They should break through during the ninth or tenth month.

By the end of the month, he probably can:

- Crawl up stairs.
- Say "mama" or "dada."
- Creep, crawl, or take a few steps with some support from you.
- Enjoy water play.
- Feed himself finger food, and he may have taste preferences.
- Respond to his name.

Encourage your baby by letting him hold on to your fingers while he practices his toddling skills. It's time to introduce more sophisticated toys with multiple parts, such as shape sorters and stacking cups. Continue to play, talk, and read to him.

MONTH TEN

Your active ten-month-old may resent being confined to a stroller or car seat. He would rather be out and about on his own and will communicate his preference loudly. Since it's not always safe or convenient to let him have his way, keep confining trips to a minimum, if possible, and offer him lots of opportunities to get around by himself. Stranger and separation anxieties are increasing, and he may show a sudden fearfulness of routines or sounds that did not bother him before: having a shirt pulled over his head, for instance, or hearing the vacuum, a siren, or a whistling teapot.

By the end of the month, he can probably:

- Stand with little support.
- Sit down from a standing position.
- Roll a ball.
- Pretend to talk on a toy telephone.
- Play "Peek-a-boo" himself.
- Search for an object if he has seen it hidden.
- Repeat sounds and gestures for attention.
- Pick up very small objects between thumb and forefinger.

Encourage your baby by being tactful and gentle when dealing with fears. Give reassuring hugs, and don't force him to touch or handle a feared object. In time his fears will dissipate.

MONTH ELEVEN

Sometime during the eleventh month, your baby will probably start walking, holding on to furniture for support. Cruising, as it is called, is soon followed by a baby's first independent step. Let your baby cruise barefoot indoors for the best possible traction.

By the end of the month, he can probably:

- Make long babbling sentences that are fully inflected.
- Say one word other than "mama" or "dada."
- Hold out his arm or leg to help you dress him.
- Drop objects for someone else to pick up.
- Drink independently from a cup.
- Understand simple commands such as "Bring me the book" or "Hug the teddy."
- Take a step without holding on to anything.

Encourage your baby by showing your appreciation when he helps out at dressing time. Take falls in stride by saying "uh-oh" instead of "oh no." Now is a good time to introduce a stable riding toy.

MONTH TWELVE

Your twelve-month-old may seem like a perpetual-motion machine, but his attention span for quiet activities is also increasing. Now might be a good time to introduce longer picture books. He may also concentrate for as long as fifteen minutes on an activity such as emptying out and playing with the contents of a laundry basket. Your baby's first set of molars are beginning to erupt.

By the end of the month, he can probably:

- Give a kiss on request.
- Give and take a toy.
- Walk with or without help.
- Point to objects that he wants.
- Imitate activities of adults and older siblings, such as brushing hair, stirring with a spoon, blowing on hot food.
- Play to a crowd and repeat an action if his audience laughs.
- Enjoy pull-and-push toys.
- Scribble with a chunky crayon if you tape paper to a work surface.

Encourage your baby by applauding his determined efforts to walk independently toward your outstretched arms. Mastering this and other physical skills is your baby's top priority right now. Before you know it, he'll be off and running straight into toddlerhood.

Appendix B

Gross Motor Development Milestones[1]

Gross Motor Skill	Average Time Achieved	Normal Range	Explanation
Sitting	28-42 weeks	22-50 weeks	Child will progress from well supported with cushions for longer and longer periods to unsupported for longer periods.
Rolling over	1. From stomach to back: 14-28 weeks 2. From back to tummy: 14-30 weeks	1. 14-28 weeks 2. 14-30 weeks	The beginning of locomotion— requires gaining control of trunk of body.
Creeping	28-36 weeks	24-44 weeks	Starts to make progress by combination of creeping and crawling— progress may at first be backward.
Crawling	32-48 weeks	28-52 weeks	
Standing	18-30 weeks	14-34 weeks	Control of his posture improves, and he gradually gains strength in lower body and legs to support body weight.
Cruising	28-54 weeks		Moves around room by holding on to furniture.
Walking	36-64 wks.		Progresses from walking with hands held, on his own but falling frequently, to walking well on his own without assistance.

Gross Motor Skill	Average Time Achieved	Normal Range	Explanation
Running	Between 18-24 months	By age two, most can kick a ball forward.	Moves from walking fast to running —usually can't swerve or change course quickly.
Climbing	Beginning to show interest between 14-18 months of age		Important exercise for developing and strengthening muscles, and improving physical coordination.
Negotiating stairs	18-24 months		
Kicking a ball	Sometime after 18 months of age		Requires momentarily balancing on one foot while swinging the other foot.
Throwing	Early in the second year of life		Most throwing underhanded; by 24 months is beginning to be more adept at bending his elbow to control accuracy.

Notes

ONE
Following Our Roots

1. Virginia Satir, *Conjoint Family Therapy* (Palo Alto, Calif.: Science and Behavior Books, 1967), 50.

TWO
Welcome to the World!

1. K.S. Robson et al., "Patterns and Determinants of Maternal Attachments," *Journal of Pediatrics* 77 (1970), 976.
2. Theodore Lidz, *The Person* (New York: Basic Books, 1968), 66.
3. Lidz, 66.
4. Tom Biracree and Nancy Biracree, *The Parents' Book of Facts: Child Development from Birth to Five* (Ballantine Books, 1989), 87.
5. Mohsen Ziai, ed., *Pediatrics* (Boston: Little, Brown, 1969), 455.
6. R.A. Spitz, "Hospitalism: An Inquiry into the Genesis of Psychiatric Conditions in Early Childhood," *The Psychoanalytic Study of the Child*, vol. 1 (New York: International Universities Press, 1945), 53-74.
7. David F. Bjorklund and Barbara B. Bjorklund, "Falling in Love with Your Baby: Attachment to One's Infant Occurs at Different Times for Different Parents," *Parents Magazine* (1991), 66(8), 57.
8. L.F. Newman; J.H. Kennell; M. Klauss; J.M. Schreiber, "Early Human Interaction: Mother and Child," *Primary Care* (1976), 3, 491-505.
9. Bjorklund and Bjorklund, 57.
10. James McConnell, editor, *Understanding Human Behavior* (New York: Holt Rinehart and Winston, 1977), 503-507.

THREE
Did You Hear That?

1. Katherine Karlsrud and Dodi Schultz, "Speech in the Making," *Parents Magazine* (1988), 63(11), 240.
2. Nanette Newberg, "Your Baby's World of Sound," *Pediatrics for Parents* (February 1992), 2.
3. Newberg, 2.
4. Marjory Roberts, "No Language but a Cry," *Psychology Today* (1987), 21, 57.
5. Roberts, 57.
6. George A. Miller and Patricia M. Gildea, "How Children Learn Words," *Scientific American* (September 1987), 257(6), 94.

7. Leah Yarrow, "Babble, Coos, and Gurgles: How Babies Learn to Talk," *Parents Magazine* (1990), 65(9), 69.
8. Michael K. Meyerhoff, "Enhancing Your Child's Early Language Development," *Pediatrics for Parents,* June 1992, 6.

FOUR
Look Ma! No Hands!

1. Biracree and Biracree, 80-82.
2. Roberta Israeloff and Roy DeLamar, "First Steps," *Parents Magazine,* 1991, 66(7), 53.
3. Israeloff and DeLamar, 53.
4. P. Leach, *Your Baby and Child* (New York: Knopf, 1993).
5. Biracree and Biracree, 153.

FIVE
Why, Mommy, Why?

1. Biracree and Biracree, 94.
2. Michael K. Meyerhoff, "Infant Stimulation Made Easy," *Pediatrics for Parents,* January 1992, 6.
3. Jean Piaget, *The Psychology of Intelligence* (London: Routledge & Kegan Paul, 1950), 191.
4. Piaget, 191.
5. Michael K. Meyerhoff, "Making Sense of Developmental Milestones," *Pediatrics for Parents,* July-August 1992, 10.
6. Biracree and Biracree, 116-17.
7. David Elkind, *The Hurried Child* (New York: Addison-Wesley), 52.

SIX
Relationship 101

1. J. Bowlby, "The Making and Breaking of Affectional Bonds, Parts I and II," *British Journal of Psychiatry,* 1977, 130, 201-10.
2. Cindy Hazan and Philip Shaver, "Romantic Love Conceptualized as an Attachment Process," *Journal of Personality & Social Psychology,* 1987, 52(3) 511-24.
3. The Brown University Child and Adolescent Behavior Letter, November 1991, 7(11), 5.
4. Hazan and Shaver, 511-24.
5. Hazan and Shaver, 520.
6. Hazan and Shaver, 522.
7. A. Bandura, D. Ross, and S.A. Ross, "Imitation of Film-Mediated Aggressive Models," *Journal of Abnormal and Social Psychology* 1963, 66, 3-11.
8. Erik Erikson, *Childhood and Society* (New York: Norton, 1963), 248.
9. Erikson, 250.
10. Erikson, 254.

SEVEN
Feelings?... What Feelings?

1. Roberta Israeloff, "What It Feels Like to Be... Two," *Parents Magazine,* September 1991, 84.
2. Erik Erikson, *Childhood and Society* (New York: Norton, 1963), 255.
3. B. Weissbourd, "Cultivating Self-esteem," *Parents Magazine,* 67 (1), 110.

EIGHT
Look Who's Talking!

1. Biracree and Biracree, 94.

NINE
These Shoes Are Made for Walking (and Running)!

1. Biracree and Biracree, 200.

TEN
Reality—What a Concept!

1. James Harnish, ed. James S. Hewett, *Illustrations Unlimited* (Wheaton, Ill.: Tyndale House, 1988), 412.
2. B.E. Jordan, N. Radin, and A. Epstein, "Paternal Behavior and Intellectual Functioning in Preschool Boys and Girls," *Developmental Psychology,* 11 (3), 1975, 407-8.
3. S. Svanum, R.G. Bringle, J.E. McLaughlin, "Father Absence and Cognitive Performance in a Large Sample of Six- to Eleven-year-old Children," *Child Development,* 53 (3), 1982, 136-43.

ELEVEN
Me, You, and Us

1. Elkind, 122.

TWELVE
Did I Do Something Wrong?

1. W. Damon, *The Moral Child: Nurturing Children's Natural Moral Growth* (New York: MacMillan, 1988), 3.
2. P.D. Meier, *Christian Child-Rearing and Personality Development* (Grand Rapids: Baker, 1977), 91.
3. Damon, 10.
4. L. Kohlberg, "The Development of Moral Character and Moral Ideology," in M. L. Hoffman and L. W. Hoffman, eds., *Review of Child Development Research,* vol. 1, (New York: Russell Sage, 1964), 122.
5. Kohlberg, 122.
6. Barbara Berg, "Learning Right from Wrong," *Parents Magazine,* 1990, 65 (3), 97.

7. M. Hoffman, "Development of Prosocial Motivation: Empathy and Guilt," in N. Eisenberg, ed., *The Development of Prosocial Behavior* (New York: Academic Press, 1982), 56.
8. Gary Collins, *Man in Transition: The Psychology of Human Development* (Carol Stream, Ill.: Creation House, 1971), 53.
9. Berg, 97.

APPENDIX A
A Month-by-Month Tour of Your Newborn

1. Dena K. Salmon, "First-year Milestones: A Month-by-Month Guide to Your Baby's Development," *Parents Magazine,* June 1992, 67(6), 97(4).

APPENDIX B
Gross Motor Development Milestones

1. Biracree, culled from *The Parents' Book of Facts* and placed in a table for consolidation purposes.